Building Apps for the Universal Windows Platform

Explore Windows 10 Native, IoT, HoloLens, and Xamarin

Ayan Chatterjee

Apress®

Building Apps for the Universal Windows Platform

Ayan Chatterjee
Swindon, Wiltshire, United Kingdom

ISBN-13 (pbk): 978-1-4842-2628-5   ISBN-13 (electronic): 978-1-4842-2629-2
DOI 10.1007/978-1-4842-2629-2

Library of Congress Control Number: 2017946340

Cover image designed by Freepik.

Managing Director: Welmoed Spahr
Editorial Director: Todd Green
Acquisitions Editor: Celestin Suresh John
Development Editor: Laura Berendson
Technical Reviewer: Manish Sharma
Coordinating Editor: Sanchita Mandal
Copy Editor: Mary Behr
Compositor: SPi Global
Indexer: SPi Global
Artist: SPi Global

Distributed to the book trade worldwide by Springer Science+Business Media New York, 233 Spring Street, 6th Floor, New York, NY 10013. Phone 1-800-SPRINGER, fax (201) 348-4505, e-mail orders-ny@springer-sbm.com, or visit www.springeronline.com. Apress Media, LLC is a California LLC and the sole member (owner) is Springer Science + Business Media Finance Inc (SSBM Finance Inc). SSBM Finance Inc is a **Delaware** corporation.

For information on translations, please e-mail rights@apress.com, or visit www.apress.com/rights-permissions.

Apress titles may be purchased in bulk for academic, corporate, or promotional use. eBook versions and licenses are also available for most titles. For more information, reference our Print and eBook Bulk Sales web page at www.apress.com/bulk-sales.

Any source code or other supplementary material referenced by the author in this book is available to readers on GitHub via the book's product page, located at www.apress.com/978-1-4842-2628-5. For more detailed information, please visit www.apress.com/source-code.

Printed on acid-free paper

To all who, at some point in their lives, rebelled against every single thing they had and dreamt of making them better.

Contents at a Glance

Contents

About the Author

Ayan Chatterjee has over four years of experience developing for Windows Store, five years of research, and is personally involved with Windows Store for Business (previously known as MSADP within Microsoft). He holds a Master of Technology in Computer Science and has contributed to several enterprises involved with Windows Store.

Follow Ayan on Twitter at @apphub365 or LinkedIn at www.linkedin.com/in/ayanprofile/.

About the Technical Reviewer

Manish Sharma is a Senior Technology Evangelist at Microsoft. He has 14 years of experience with various organizations and is primarily involved in technological enhancements.

He is an expert in data (Lucene, Solr, MongoDB, Cassandra, DocumentDB, Elastic Search, MarkLogic, Azure Search, etc.) and cloud (Azure, AWS, SoftLayer, OpenStack, etc.) technologies. Most recently he worked on .NET, UWP, client-server architecture-based applications, SOA integration projects, and helping ISVs (software product organizations) to optimize their applications on Microsoft Azure.

He has expertise in telecom and has exposure with various other domains like BFSI, commodity trading, and retail.

He is a certified Azure Solution Architect, Cloud Data Architect, .NET Solution Developer, and PMP Certified Project Manager. He is a regular speaker at various technical conferences organized by Microsoft (FutureDecoded, Azure Conference, and specialized webinars) and community events (GIDS, Docker, etc.) for client-server, cloud, and data technologies.

He is an author at *Open Source For You* (OSFY) magazine.

Follow Manish on Twitter at @manisharma_ms or LinkedIn at www.linkedin.com/in/mannu2050/.

Introduction

When I sat down to author this book, I thought about how to make everything simple. In my school days, the books were full of definitions and technical explanations which made a lot of people say "I don't speak computer." The purpose of this book is to give you the core values and the core concepts embedded into a technology so you get a natural flow of thought while building your application. I look at the evolution in the world of computing and how it all fits together. The initial concern was how to make things work. Today, the tools of the trade work behind the scenes, hiding behind the main goal of the work and the things most important. A writer or a student should not care whether his/her content is authored in Microsoft Word or Apple Pages or LaTeX as long as the writing experience fits organically into the author's flow and the document created can be opened and read (compatible) by other people using other software. In other words, the tools should fit seamlessly into an individual's workflow.

UWP fits this bill in a developer's workflow: the developed application can reach a range of devices, be it personal devices (like Surface Laptop, Surface Pro, Surface Book) to devices in an enterprise to the IoT, and even to other operating systems like iOS and Android, all of them using the same language and, in most cases, the same lines of code.

This book covers the robust use and the core concepts in UWP. Explanations are made as simple as possible, comparing concepts with real-world situations. The first two chapters cover the most basic concepts, incrementing the level of understanding slowly as your understanding of UWP grows with each chapter, culminating with the publication process on the app store. This book fulfills its purpose if, by the end of your learning process, you are able to build complex, enterprise-level applications for your school, your job, your company, or even as a hobby.

CHAPTER 1

■ ■ ■

Introduction to Windows Universal

Any business aims to maximize profits and minimize the manufacturing costs without compromising the quality of the product. For an application, the way to maximize profits is through an increase in downloads. One of the ways to achieve this is by introducing your application to more than one platform. By reusing code, you can speed up the development process. In summary, the goal is to distribute your application to as many platforms as possible and to reduce the hours it takes to reach this goal.

Windows Store applications are the successor to Windows Presentation Foundation (WPF) applications. And WPF applications are the successor to Windows Forms applications. Each succession has resulted in a new user interface. In this chapter, you will explore some of the elements in a Windows application in brief. In later chapters, you will take a deeper dive into components and features specific to the Universal Windows Platform (UWP). The most common and widely used elements are

1. **Button**

   The button is one of the most elementary controls. A Button control is designed to be clicked. The following XAML code demonstrates the use of a button:

   ```
   <Button x:Name="ClickButton1">Click Me</Button>
   ```

   In metro applications, you have the option to pick a regular button or an app bar button whose XAML looks like

   ```
   <AppBarButton Icon="Play" Label="Play Me"
   Click="PlayMe_Click"/>
   ```

2. **TextBlock**

   The text block is mainly used for headings and text otherwise not intended for users to edit.

   XAML example:

   ```
   <TextBlock Name="textBlock1">Heading 1</TextBlock>
   ```

© Ayan Chatterjee 2017
A. Chatterjee, *Building Apps for the Universal Windows Platform*,
DOI 10.1007/978-1-4842-2629-2_1

■ **Tip**   Visual Studio and Blend have a search option whereby you may search for any control.

---

3. **TextBox**

    Unlike a text block, a text box is designed for text input from
    the user. It can be a single line or multiline and can perform
    advanced character masking such as password inputs. A text
    box can also be used for longer text that does not require
    editing and input such as terms and conditions of a signup
    page. To restrict editing, the IsReadOnly property is set to true.
    The input text can be recovered with the Text property.

    XAML example:

    ```
    <TextBox x:Name="PasswordBox" />
    ```

    To read the input from this TextBox, the syntax is
    PasswordBox.Text.

4. **Slider**

    Sliders are used to offer a range of values for the user to slide
    such as zoom, shopping price range, feedback rating, etc.

    XAML example:

    ```
    <Slider Header="Volume" ValueChanged="Slider_
    ValueChanged"/>
    ```

5. **Check Box**

    The check box is used to select or deselect single or multiple
    items.

    XAML example:

    ```
    <CheckBox Content="Close all Tabs" x:Name="CloseTabs"/>
    ```

6. **Radio Button**

    Radio buttons are used for multiple options that are mutually
    exclusive (the user needs to pick only one).

    XAML example:

    ```
    <RadioButton Content="Male" Tag="Male" Checked="Male_
    Checked"/>
    <RadioButton Content="Female" Tag="Female"
    Checked="Female_Checked"/>
    ```

You will notice that there are two things with the same value in this context: Content and Tag. Although not required in this scenario, the Tag property is put in place to show its use. A Tag has no default value but it can be used to put additional properties in the radio button such as data binding to an image, meaning you can put an image or even an animation instead of just text.

7. **Toggle Switch**

   The toggle switch is built to resemble a physical switch such as turning on/off Wi-Fi, turning on/off Touch on the phone, etc.

   XAML example:

   ```
   <ToggleSwitch x:Name="TVSwitchToggle" Header="TV"/>
   ```

8. **Image**

   An Image control represents an image and its source can be set as a Uniform Resource Identifier (URI) from which an image is loaded. A URI can either be a local resource or a web resource. With Windows 10, Image now supports GIF animations.

   XAML syntax:

   ```
   <Image Source="URI"/>
   ```

   The Image.Stretch property determines how an image is displayed. It can be one of the four possible choices– none, fill, uniform, and uniform to fill. An example of assigning a Stretch property within C# is

   ```
   myImage.Stretch = Stretch.Fill;
   ```

   where myImage is your image object.

   None will present the content in its original size. Fill will resize the image to fit the width and height of the image control. Uniform will resize to the image control, keeping the aspect ratio fixed. UniformToFill will resize to fit the dimensions of the image control and crop the overflown region. For instance, consider an image of 800x800 pixels and an image control of 1000x900 pixels. None will keep the image at 800x800, Fill will make it 1000x900, Uniform will make it 900x900, and UniformToFill will make it 1000x1000 and crop the overflown region.

9. **Lists**

   Lists show a collection of objects such as contact list. The four most widely used lists are list views, grid views, drop-down lists, and list boxes.

   XAML example:

   ```
   <ListView>
               Items
   </ListView>
   ```

10. **Grid**

    Grids are used to distribute child elements to rows and columns inside the grid according to their row/column arrangements.

    XAML example:

    ```
    <Grid>
            Elements
    </Grid>
    ```

11. **Canvas**

    A canvas defines an area where you can have child elements and position them using coordinates that are relative to the canvas area. Prior to Windows 10 Inking, applications built for sketching and painting were built using canvas.

    XAML example:

    ```
    <Canvas>
                    Elements
    </Canvas>
    ```

■ **Note**   You may notice that some elements have x:Name while others have just Name. Note that x: is used to make the element globally available.

Windows 10 and UWP

Windows 10 was launched globally on July 29, 2015. With Windows 10, there is a union between desktop, mobile, holographic, wearables, Xbox, and IoTs. We will be using Microsoft Visual C# among other languages for the code behind and Extensible Markup

Language (XAML) for the front end. If you are new to app development, moving forward with C# will be of great benefit since

- It is widely used since Windows Forms.

- It is more type safe.

- It has a wide range of code samples and libraries available.

- It can be reused in Xamarin to build for iOS, macOS, and Android.

Figure 1-1 shows a teenager visiting an eye clinic after sunset and getting his regular human eyes replaced with another version of eyes that support night vision. With the Anniversary Update on August 2016 and the Creators Update of 2017, Windows 10 gets incremented the same way: one component at a time. To better understand this growth, we shall take a peek into the past and see how Windows development has progressed over the years.

Figure 1-1. *Comic Demonstrating an update*

We have all heard about the "One Windows" goal, or build once, deploy on all. While that is the long-term vision, let's understand this goal by looking at the growth in deployment of built applications. Let's see the history of application development.

1. **One for One**

   Traditionally, applications and games were built in fixed dimensions. As a developer, you would start building with width and height, or with a constant aspect ratio. The hardware was built accordingly by hardware manufacturers.

2. **One for Many**

   Then came a time when we could build for multiple aspect ratios and sizes. This gave rise to a new era of apps where we could create a solution for one OS (phone, desktop, Xbox, and so on) no matter the screen size. Of course, there were limitations but we had room for further growth and flexibility.

If you are familiar with the Windows 8 family of app development and you are building for both phone and desktop, you create one project for Windows and another for Windows Phone. A shared component could exist where you could write shared code. Still, this was not the ideal way to build. Figure 1-2 shows a Windows 8.1 solution and separate projects for Windows, Windows Phone, and the shared components.

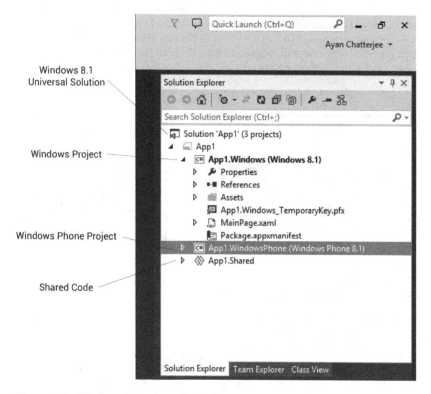

Figure 1-2. *Windows 8.1 universal solution*

3. **One for All**

With Windows 10, you can now cross that barrier and build one universal solution for all types of Windows 10 devices. Instead of writing shared code, today you need to write only once. See Figure 1-3.

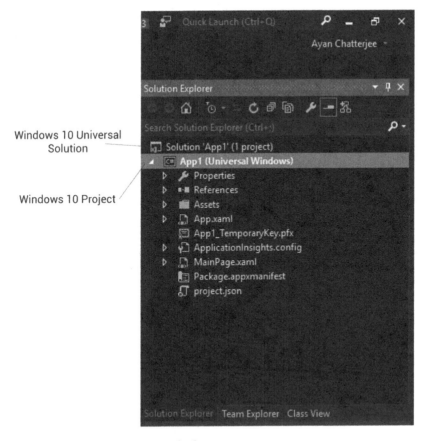

Windows 10 Universal
Solution

Windows 10 Project

Figure 1-3. *Windows 10 universal solution*

.NET Languages and Architecture

Let's consider a class in a school. You are mentoring in a home for orphans and it has a heterogeneous demographic. Your task is to grade some essays. You have the essays of four of the students: Jack C, Rohan C++, Robin HTML5, and Lily C#. They have each written their essay in their native language, so you have essays in four different languages to evaluate. You can simply open a translator application and get them translated to English. This is what happens in a .NET environment. No matter what programming language is picked, the related compiler and linker will get it translated to an intermediate language for processing. This is one of the major benefits of .NET.

Windows 10 and Universal Windows Applications are created on a platform-homogeneous architecture. This means a developer need not recode the application to support different platforms of Windows 10. Presently, for UWP applications the following four languages are widely used for code behind:

- C++

- C#

- Microsoft Visual Basic

- WinJS

Installing Visual Studio and Components

Prior to building and deploying UWP applications, it is a good practice to enable the developer mode on your device. Windows then grants you permission to deploy locally built applications that have not yet acquired Windows Store licenses. Just like a corporate official needs proper identification (biometric, ID card, etc.) to enter a corporate building, Windows checks for a license before installing an application. Among other things, it verifies whether the app originates from a registered developer in Windows Store and that the app meets the safety and security rules of Windows Store. Figure 1-4 shows how you can enable developer mode from Settings.

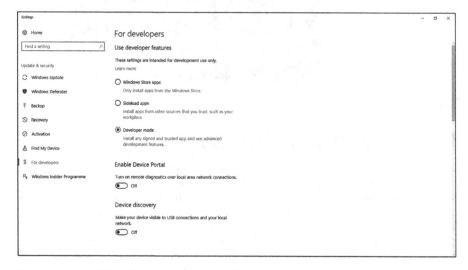

Figure 1-4. *Enabling developer mode on Windows 10*

There are several choices to obtain Visual Studio and several editions of Visual Studio available on the market (see Figure 1-5). The three most widely used are the following:

- **Visual Studio Community**

  Community is presently free and covers most of the development essentials that one would need to build a UWP application.

- **Visual Studio Professional**

  Professional contains some added features such as Team Foundation Server features and differs a bit by removing restrictions.

- **Visual Studio Enterprise**

  Enterprise is made for professionals who wish to collaborate and work on a team to make incredibly complex projects. Windows Store presently defines an enterprise organization as having more than 250 devices or an organization that produces greater than 1 million US dollars in annual revenue.

Figure 1-5. Different editions of Visual Studio 2017

■ **Note**   You must have Visual Studio 2015 or later, Blend for Visual Studio, and Universal App Development Tools installed to build applications for Windows 10.

The edition you pick depends on your requirements. If you use a Macintosh computer and not a Windows machine, you can still install Windows 10 on a virtual machine to make use of Visual Studio. One great way to use Windows on a macOS device is through third-party applications such as VMWare or Parallels Desktop (shown in Figure 1-6). Another choice is Bootcamp (shown in Figure 1-7 and built by Apple); it provides a great way to partition a macOS drive and install Windows.

Figure 1-6. *Parallels Desktop Control Center post Windows installation*

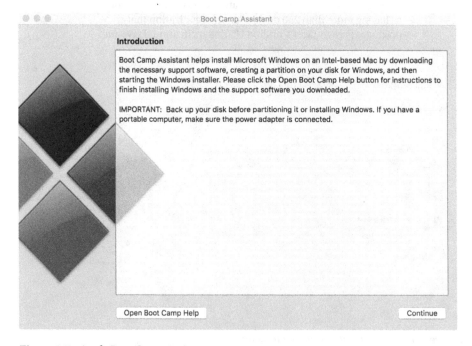

Figure 1-7. *Apple Boot Camp Assistant start page*

Now let's proceed with the Visual Studio installation. There are several ways to acquire Visual Studio. If you are a Microsoft Developer Network (MSDN) subscribed member, installation discs and ISO files of Visual Studio are readily available for download. Those with moderate or high speed Internet may opt to download and install Visual Studio from the installer available on the Microsoft website.

■ **Tip**   Along with Blend for Visual Studio, its predecessor, Microsoft Expression Blend, is a Paint-like application and is powerful and useful for many occasions to create custom-defined shapes in XAML.

The following are the steps to install Visual Studio:

1. Run the installer.

2. Make sure that **Universal Windows App Development Tools** is checked (Figure 1-8 and Figure 1-9 for Visual Studio 2015 and 2017, respectively).

3. If your edition supports it and you wish to expand your market to Apple and Android devices, check **Xamarin**.

4. Wait until the installer completes (Figure 1-10 for Professional edition and Figure 1-11 for Community edition). It may take several minutes to several hours to complete. Different editions of Visual Studio are shown in Figures 1-8 through 1-11 to show their similarity.

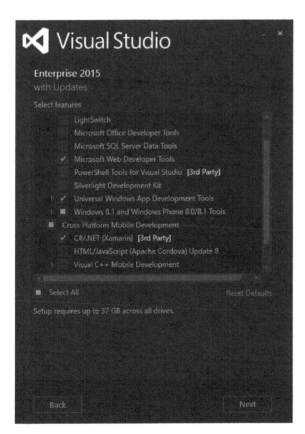

Figure 1-8. Installing Visual Studio Enterprise 2015

11

Figure 1-9. *Installing Visual Studio Professional 2017*

Figure 1-10. *Visual Studio 2017 Professional installation process*

Figure 1-11. *Visual Studio 2017 Community installation process*

UWP and Cross-Platform Xamarin

You read earlier in this chapter of the positive and negative components of development. One positive is to reduce development time. Xamarin will help you extend your app's audience from Windows to iOS, macOS (formally known as OS X), and Android. The development part is covered in Chapter 9 of the book, so for now I shall only cover the installation. Much like Visual Studio, one may download the installation components separately and install offline or use the online installer. If you do not have high speed Internet, I recommend using the offline method.

In earlier versions of Visual Studio 2015, if you used higher tiers of Visual Studio such as Visual Studio Enterprise, Xamarin came with the package so you have already installed it along with the rest of the components. For Visual Studio 2017, you can install Xamarin straightaway on the first run. For those who do not wish to, Xamarin Studio installer is easily available on Xamarin website. You have the option to install Xamarin Studio on your Windows machine if you are using one, or on a Macintosh machine; Xamarin is available for both platforms. Figure 1-12 shows the installer on a Macintosh machine.

Figure 1-12. Xamarin Installer on macOS

Setting Up a New Project

Now that you have successfully installed Visual Studio and Windows SDK, you shall take the first step towards the development of a fully functional application named Color Architect. For the next couple of chapters, you shall build this application bit by bit while learning the elements of Windows 10. The name Color Architect is inspired by architects who design the interior and exterior of magnificent buildings. Similarly, you shall use mathematical operations on colors in RGB to build a new color.

Before creating a new project, let's understand the concepts of a *minimum* and *target version*. These are coined TargetPlatformVersion and TargetPlatformMinVersion in a project's settings. The target version is the maximum version number the application has been tested in and the minimum target version is the minimum Windows 10 version the application supports. They can be the same or different.

Just like TargetPlatformMinVersion specifies the minimum version of Windows 10 required to run the application, every Visual Studio solution has a MinVSVersion property that specifies the version of Visual Studio a solution was created in and the version that the solution can support.

Now that all of the tools have been set up, you can begin by creating a blank application project with the following steps:

1. Open Visual Studio 2017.

2. Click **New Project** from the Start Page under File in menu bar (Figure 1-13).

3. In New Project options, click **Blank App (Universal Windows)** (Figure 1-14).

4. Depending on the version of the SDK installed on your device, it may ask for a minimum and target platform version (Figure 1-15).

5. You are good to go!

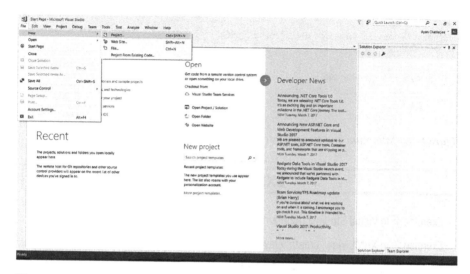

Figure 1-13. *Visual Studio 2017 Community home page*

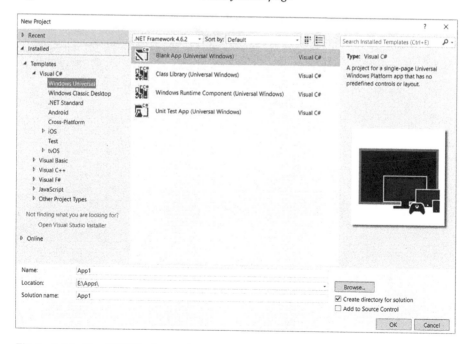

Figure 1-14. *New UWP Project options*

15

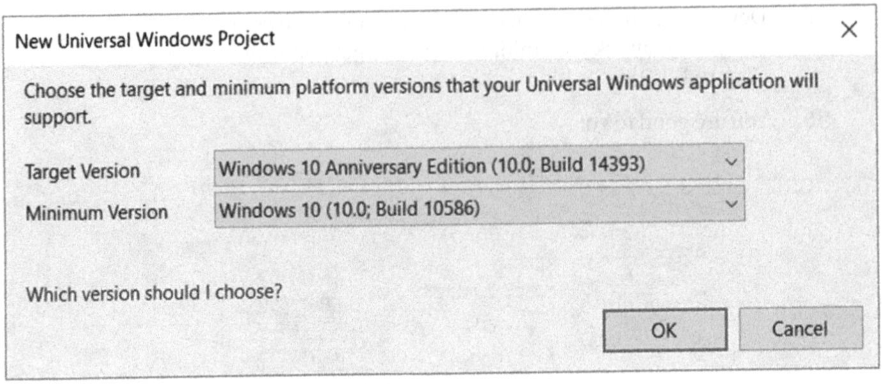

New Universal Windows Project   ×

Choose the target and minimum platform versions that your Universal Windows application will support.

Target Version   Windows 10 Anniversary Edition (10.0; Build 14393)   ⌄

Minimum Version   Windows 10 (10.0; Build 10586)   ⌄

Which version should I choose?

                                                        OK   Cancel

Figure 1-15. Minimum and target version selection

EXERCISES

Exercise 1: In Visual Studio, create a new Windows Store Application.

Exercise 2: In XAML view, create a layout of a simple calculator.

Exercise 3: Explore the properties of layout controls `TextBox`, `AppBarButton`, and `ToggleSwitch`.

Exercise 4: Explore the row and column definitions of a grid.

CHAPTER 2

Elementary Concepts

If you picked up this book, I can safely assume that you are familiar with programing. Keeping that assumption in mind, let's brush up on some concepts and take a look at their implementations in Visual Studio.

When a baby (let's say her name is Tia) sees a ball for the first time, Tia forms an image of the object in her mind along with its properties such as circular shape, size, color, and material. She has now established an object and its properties. Next, she will want to name it. If Tia's native language is not English, she shall know the ball as another name by listening to the words of her guardians and other adults around her and call a ball by that name. This helps others understand what she is talking about when she talks about a ball.

Let's now talk about identifying the different types of balls. Two different balls, such as a baseball and a basketball, are recognized in the mind by the same characteristics, namely size, color, texture, and purpose. We make the same distinction in a computer program by using a concept known as *decision boundary*.

If you have set up a new project for Color Architect, the outcome should be as shown in Figure 2-1. Let's take a quick look at colors. The RGB for white is R = 255, G = 255, B = 255 and for black is R = 0, G = 0, B = 0. When R = G = B = some value between 0 and 255, it is a shade of grey between black and white. If the values are not equal, it moves from greyscale to multiple colors. Some values of RGB are

Red: R = 255, G = 0, B = 0

Green: R = 0, G = 255, B = 0

Blue: R = 0, G = 0, B = 255

Tomato: R = 255, G = 99, B = 71

Orange: R = 255, B = 165, B = 0

Brown: R = 165, G = 42, B = 42, and so on.

© Ayan Chatterjee 2017
A. Chatterjee, *Building Apps for the Universal Windows Platform*,
DOI 10.1007/978-1-4842-2629-2_2

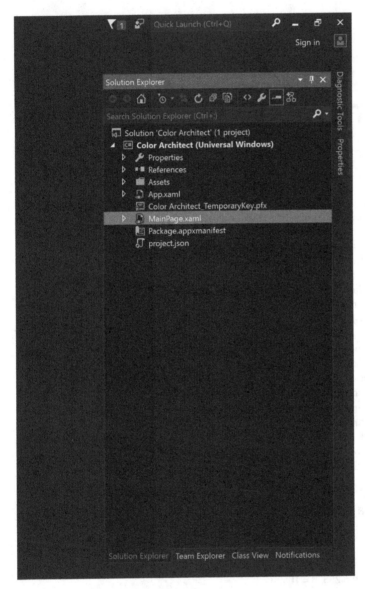

Figure 2-1. *New project for Color Architect*

Mathematical combinations of such values make up beautiful palettes. Let's make palettes of five colors with brown and the following parameters.

BETWEEN WHITE

1. Color 1: Brown (165, 42, 42)

2. Color 2:

   R = 165 + ((255-165)/(5-1)) = 165 + 22.5 = 187.5 ~ 188

   G = 42 + ((255-42)/(5-1)) = 42 + 53.25 = 95.25 ~ 95

   B = 42 + ((255–42)/(5-1)) = 42 + 53.25 = 95.25 ~ 95

3. Color 3:

   R = 165 + 45 = 210

   G = 42 + 106.5 = 148.5 ~ 149

   B = 42 + 106.5 = 148.5 ~ 149

4. Color 4:

   R = 165 + 67.5 = 232.5 ~ 233

   G = 42 + 159.75 = 201.75 ~ 202

   B = 42 + 159.75 = 201.75 ~ 202

5. Color 5: White (255, 255, 255)

BETWEEN BLACK

1. Color 1: Black (0, 0, 0)

2. Color 2:

   R = 0 + ((165-0)/(5-1)) = 41.25 ~ 41

   G = 0 + ((42-0)/(5-1)) = 10.5 ~ 11

   B = 0 + ((42-0)/(5-1)) = 10.5 ~ 11

3. Color 3:

   R = 82.5 ~ 83

   G = 21

   B = 21

4. Color 4:

   R = 123.75 ~ 124

   B = 31.5 ~ 32

   G = 31.5 ~ 32

5. Color 5: Brown (165, 42, 42)

BETWEEN TOMATO

1. Color 1: Tomato (255, 99, 71)

2. Color 2:

   R = 255 − ((255-165)/(5-1))

   G = 99 − ((99-42)/(5-1))

   B = 71 − ((71-42)/(5-1))

3. Color 3:

   R = 255 − 2*((255-165)/(5-1))

   G = 99 − 2*((99-42)/(5-1))

   B = 71 − 2*((71-42)/(5-1))

4. Color 4:

   R = 255 − 3*((255-165)/(5-1))

   G = 99 − 3*((99-42)/(5-1))

   B = 71 − 3*((71-42)/(5-1))

5. Color 5: Brown (165, 42, 42)

The example with white or black is called a monochromatic color palette as the middle colors show a lighter or darker shade, respectively. In this chapter, you shall learn to build Color Architect so that it looks like Figures 2-2 and 2-3.

■ **Tip**   Try to form general mathematical equations of such color palettes.

Figure 2-2. *Basic layout of Color Architect*

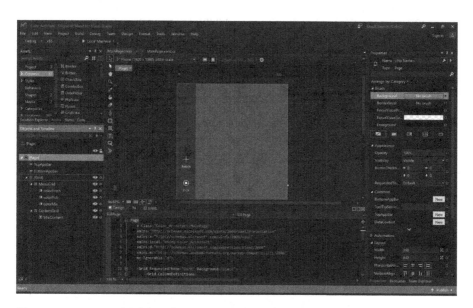

Figure 2-3. *Layout of Color Architect as seen from Blend for Visual Studio*

Object-Oriented Programing

While programing, friendly names for classes and functions help you or another programmer understand the purpose of those classes or functions. It is especially helpful when you are building a complex program with multiple function names and you are calling the function from another class. Comments also help with debugging as well.

■ **Tip** It is always a good habit to keep the function and class names simple and easy to understand.

C# provides full support for object-oriented programing including encapsulation, inheritance, and polymorphism. They may sound like big names, but we shall look at them one at a time.

Encapsulation is taking data and functions and putting them all together in a capsule (in one unit). It allows for hiding of components from the outside, so the developer needs to concern herself with working with the encapsulated component only.

Inheritance is copying the properties of a parent class to a child class. For example, let's consider the age of a human being. Age is a real number but it is not all of the real number range. A human being can live up to 110 or maybe 130 if very lucky. For arguments sake, let's say the maximum range is 150. In other words, the age of a human being inherits all existing properties of real numbers with a custom-defined range of its own.

Polymorphism is the existence of a function in several forms. *Poly* means many and *morphe* means form. What does this mean? Let's say you want to create a geometrical shape of a polygon. Let's look at some polygons with the same function name:

1. Polygon(5)

    Since only one input has been provided, it means it is a square of two equal sides.

2. Polygon(5, 7)

    Since two inputs have been provided, it means it is a rectangle with width and height.

3. Polygon(5, 7, 3)

    This polygon has three inputs, which specifies it is a three-dimensional polygon having width, height, and depth.

You can see that the same function name may have different jobs all depending on its input.

Function, Class, and Solution

Any sequence of actions that can be grouped together in one unit is a function. It is the basic task of a computer. For instance, let's say that you are going on a vacation and you wish to take your laptop with you. The following sequence of steps will occur:

1. If the laptop is on, shut down the laptop.

2. Close the lid.

3. Pick up the laptop from the desk.

4. Walk the steps to where your backpack is located.

5. Put the laptop inside the bag in an arranged manner.

These steps put together can be called a function. Let's look at how these steps form a function:

```
function packLaptop(object laptop)
{
        laptopState = laptop.isOn? Save work and shut down : do nothing;
        closeLid(laptop.type_of_laptop);
        pickUpLaptop(desk, hand);
        walk(currentPosition, nearBackpack);
        putLaptopInBag(type_of_bag);
}
```

Functions are of two types: built-in and custom defined. Even though both are made the same way, they differ in the source of their creation. To better understand this, let's consider an elegant hotel. You wake up from a long nap and you feel hungry. If you order food through room service, the hotel's management certifies the food because they are familiar with the chef and its cooking process. These are in-built functions and they come with the package. But if you are having a pizza delivered (third party) or cooking on your own (custom defined), the hotel's management is not aware of the process and hence is unable to certify the food. The benefit of reusing a built-in function is that the function has been tested thoroughly. Any bug fixes or updates to it will improve the performance of all associated applications using it.

A class is a group of similar functions. Let's look at what the class algebra can consist of:

```
class algebra
{

function addition(numbers)
        {
                //code
        }
        function subtraction(numbers)
        {
                //code
        }
```

```
    function multiplication(numbers)
    {
            //code
    }
    function division(numbers)
    {
            //code
    }
    function percentage(numbers)
    {
            //code
    }
}
```

Similar to classes, a solution is your entire program and consists of several classes, functions, and other components. Let's take a look at the solution named mathematics:

```
namespace mathematics
{
     class algebra
     class geometry
     class trigonometry
     class calculus
     function newInventedTheorem(numbers)
}
```

Let's explore namespace now. By definition, it is used to declare a scope of related objects such as other namespaces, classes, interfaces, etc. To explain this in simple terms, I shall use the concept of multiverse. If you are not a physics or astronomy fan, or you haven't read superhero comics, a multiverse is a hypothetical possibility that multiple universes exist at the same time. The namespace declaration would be

```
namespace universe1
{
     class earth1
     {
             static void someCountry()
             {
                     //Some code
             }
     }
}
namespace universe2
{
```

```
        class earth2
        {
                static void someCountry()
                {
                        //Some code
                }
        }
}
namespace universe3
{
        class earth3
        {
                static void someCountry()
                {
                        //Some code
                }
        }
}
```

To access earth in universe1 you would call universe1.earth1.someCountry. One use of namespace is to avoid conflicts between functions of the same name defined by different teams in an organization. If you are using a simple UWP solution, you don't need to use a namespace. Apart from this, a UWP solution usually consists of the following:

- Assets (images)

- Localizable strings for the application to be available in multiple native languages

- Registration components and license information

- A database

- Package manifest for registering live tile images, supported device orientations, device capabilities the application uses such as the Internet, and so on

- Dependencies such as third-party packages like nugget or references

Conditional Statements and Loops

Conditional statements are a minimum of two steps, where the second step occurs due to a certain condition of the first. For instance, the choice to purchase a new car will entirely depend on the limit of a person's wallet.

If-else and the Conditional Operator

To put this in a standard programing syntax

```
if(condition)
{
        statement
}
else
{
        Statement
}
```

An example of this is

```
if (wallet contains $$$$)
{
        purchase a super cool sports car;
}
else {
        purchase a lame old car;
}
```

The condition part is a Boolean variable. This means that the condition part answers the question "Has the condition been met?" and the response can either be true/yes when the condition is satisfied or false/no when the condition is not satisfied. There is no room for middle value between yes or no. When a condition is not satisfied, it goes to the else section whose formal statement looks like

```
if(condition)
{
        true statement;
}
else
{
        false statement;
}
```

This, in programing terms, is called if-else. It is in our nature to be lazy. To honor this laziness, we have something to replace typing if-else all the time, which is called the conditional operator (?:). Notice the same if-else statement to purchase a car can be reduced to one line, as in

```
purchase = wallet contains $$$$? super cool sports car : lame old family car;
```

and the formal statement looks like

```
result = condition? true statement : false statement;
```

Switch Case

To avoid layers of if-else statements, there's something called a switch case. If you are not using a home automation system and are used to the traditional switchboards, you'll understand its significance right away; you walk up to the switchboard to turn on the lights and fans you want directly. Let's look at an extensive if else statement and how it can be reduced by a switch:

```
if(time == morning)
{
         have breakfast;
}
else if(time == way to work)
{
         take away a cup of coffee;
}
else if(time == lunchbreak)
{
         have lunch;
}
else if(time == afternoon)
{
         have a snack with tea/coffee/chocolate milk;
}
else if(time == evening)
{
         have dinner;
}
else if(time == midnight)
{
         have some midnight snack;
}
```

All of this code can be replaced by

```
switch(time)
{
      case morning:
             breakfast;
             break;
      case way to work:
             take away a cup of coffee;
             break;
      case lunchbreak:
             have lunch;
             break;
      case afternoon:
             have a snack with tea/coffee/chocolate milk;
```

```
            break;
    case evening:
            have dinner;
            break;
    case midnight:
            have some midnight snack;
            break;
    default:
            it's not time to eat;
}
```

You might have noticed that there is a break in every case and a default at the end. Note that default is an optional parameter that the switch goes to if and only if none of the other case conditions match. If a default is not given and there is no case match, the pointer exits the switch-case block automatically.

A switch-case block has fall down property. What this means is if there's a case match and the pointer enters the case, it does not stop. It executes all the lines in that case and all other cases below it. To prevent this, you can use a break. You can use the fall down property to your advantage as well. For instance, in the above switch-case block, coffee is common for two cases: way to work and afternoon. If you wish to take advantage of the fall down property, you may reduce the number of lines further. This way, when the pointer executes the afternoon case, it executes the way to work case and gets the user the cup of coffee.

```
switch(time)
{
    case morning:
            breakfast;
            break;
    case afternoon:
            have a snack;
    case way to work:
            get a cup of coffee;
            break;
    case lunchbreak:
            have lunch;
            break;
    case evening:
            have dinner;
            break;
    case midnight:
            have some midnight snack;
            break;
    default:
            it's not time to eat;
}
```

A loop is a set of repetitive actions. To understand its uniqueness, think of an analog watch face. The hour hand goes from 12 to 1 to 2, circling back to 12. It goes round and round in a circle (loop) until the watch breaks or its battery runs out. The breaking of the analog watch to stop the loop is an exit condition. Without an exit condition, a loop would run forever, making the program bad for the system. Such loops are called infinite loops. We shall look at the following kinds of loops:

1. for loop

2. while (and do while) loop

For Loop

A for loop is generally used when you know the definite amount of times the loop is supposed to run prior to its initialization. The standard statement of a for loop goes like

```
for (initializer, condition, iterator)
{
        Body
}
```

The same can be rewritten for simple understanding as

```
for(start, finish, iterate)
{
        Body
}
```

The initializer part is meant to initialize the control variable. If you wish to run a loop 10 times, the loop goes like

```
for(int I = 1; I<=10; I++)
```

While (and Do-While) Loops

In fact, while and do-while are similar to for loops except that they are meant for when you do not know how many times the loop is supposed to run prior to its execution. The statement goes like

```
while(condition)
{
        Body
}
```

On the other hand, a do-while loop is meant to run the loop at least once. Thus, the condition part comes at the end:

```
do
{
        Body
} while(condition);
```

Now to play a little bit, let's convert a for loop to a while loop:

<u>For</u>

```
for(int I = 1; I<=10; I++)
{
        Body
}
```

<u>While</u>

```
int I = 1;
while(I<=10)
{
        Body;
        I++;
}
```

Data Types

If you think about it, the types of data you use in your everyday life when talking or writing an email are

- Numbers

- Alphabets

- Special characters

A combination of these data types makes up the entire dictionary of our language. For a programing language, such data types are represented mainly by character and numerical data types, each having their own individual properties. The type of data used depends entirely on the situation. One such common property is the ability to perform mathematical operations. Although phone numbers are generally numerical data, you would not want to perform a mathematical operation on them, like add Dad's number and Mom's number and call some random person.

Numbers

For numbers, there are integers and floating point numbers. Integers are numbers without decimals whereas floating point numbers consist of numbers with decimal values. They can be signed or unsigned, meaning with or without the capability to hold negative numbers. Even though int is most widely used, other integer types include

- byte
- short
- int
- long

And the floating point numbers include

- float
- double
- decimal

Note that double is more widely used. Since floating point numbers are real numbers, you cannot move back and forth between integers and floating point numbers just like that. You need to perform something known as *type casting* or *type conversion*. Even in mathematics, when you convert integer 15 to a double, you can do it automatically (implicit conversion) by including decimal points 15.0 but the reverse needs some work. Let's say you now have a double value of 15.5 and you need to make it an integer. There comes a dilemma (explicit conversion) to decide if it should be 15 or 16, and there is another set of rules to solve the problem.

Explicit conversion is written as

```
(type) data
```

For example,

```
int a = 15;
double a1 = a;
double b = 15.5;
int b1 = (int) b;
```

■ **Tip**   Take a deeper look into **Convert** and **TryParse** for more detailed explicit type casting.

Alphabets and Special Characters

To store alphabets, there are characters and string literals. Character or char holds a single character whereas string can hold multiples such as a sentence or a paragraph. Example:

```
char a = 'p';
string b = "pee";
```

Now that you have learned to represent a single data type, how can a school store the names/string values of 20,000 students? Storing them in individual variable names will take forever, not to mention the confusion when the school needs to recall the variable name at a later time. This problem is solved using an array. An *array* is a lot (homogeneous mixture) of the same datatype. To represent 20,000 students, the school creates

```
String[] students = new string[20000];
```

Arrays start from 0, meaning that this students array consist of 20,000 numbers from 0 to 19,999. When the school needs to read or write to a particular data, the code will look like

```
students[10] = "Bob";
```

for the 11th student in the array.

Now that you have learned the basics, let's explore the polygon example and put it into code. You are going to use a console application just to test out the theory. Let's see the C# code for it:

C#

```csharp
using System;
namespace PolymorphismConsoleDemo
{
    class Program
    {
        static void Main(string[] args)
        {
            int square = 5;
            int[] rectangle = { 10, 5 };
            int[] box = { 10, 5, 2 };
            double areaSquare = polygon(square);
            double areaRectangle = polygon(rectangle);
            double volumeBox = polygon(box);
            Console.WriteLine("Area of square is " + areaSquare);
            Console.WriteLine("Area of rectangle is " + areaRectangle);
            Console.WriteLine("Volume of box is " + volumeBox);
```

```
        Console.ReadKey(); //to prevent the console from closing
        immediately
    }
    private static double polygon(params int[] dimensions)
    {
        int len = dimensions.Length;
        if(len == 1)
        {
            return dimensions[0] * dimensions[0];
        }
        if(len == 2)
        {
            return dimensions[0] * dimensions[1];
        }
        if(len == 3)
        {
            return dimensions[0] * dimensions[1] * dimensions[2];
        }
        return -1;
    }
}
}
```

The output is shown in Figure 2-4.

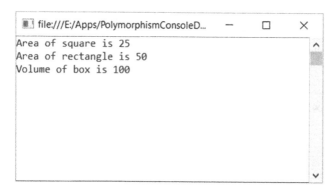

Figure 2-4. *Output of PolymorphismConsoleDemo console application*

You can see that from a single function called polygon areas of the square and rectangle as well as the volume of a box was obtained, thus exhibiting the behaviours of polymorphism. The params keyword in C# enables a function to take in multiple numbers of input arguments. The function can also execute when no argument is passed to it. The length of the params list will then be zero.

Application Life Cycle

Application life cycle is what happens and what can happen from opening the application to closing it. For this explanation, you are going to learn about the daily cycle of a working professional, Bob. Bob gets up early to brush his teeth, shave, take a shower, and eat a healthy breakfast. Then he puts on a nice professional suit to head off to work. This part of his day consists of preparations for the start of his working day. For a UWP application, this part is handled by OnLaunched method whose syntax is

```
protected virtual void OnLaunched(LaunchActivatedEventArgs args)
```

Now that Bob is prepared to go to work, he must take all the necessary files required for the day and recall any meetings or presentation he has today. When he is ready, he heads off to work. For an application, every page gets an OnNavigatedTo method to be prepared to load anything necessary and navigation requests while preparing a page for display. The syntax is

```
protected virtual void OnNavigatedTo(NavigationEventArgs e)
```

Similarly, during exit, the OnNavigatedFrom function is used.

Sharing Code

In the previous generation of the Windows 8 family, there was a separate project for shared components. However, for Windows 10 and UWP, you can do it under one roof. To share a function with another class, you need to make it globally accessible. You can achieve that by making it public and static. For Color Architect, let's create a defaults class to store the option selected by a user: fetch, pick, or mix, as shown in Figure 2-5.

Figure 2-5. *Shared code for Color Architect*

To access this from any other class in the solution, you need to first include the path of the class at the header such as

```
using Color_Architect.CustomCode;
```

and then the variable option can be called by using defaults.option or <class name>.<static variable name>.

Note that get and set are optional parameters. They show what can be accessed from the variable. To make it read-only (if you do not want someone else modifying the values of the variable outside of the program) setting it private solves that issue. Let's compare the two:

a. `public static byte option{ get; set; }`

   Calling it outside defaults.option gives the value.

   Changing defaults.option outside writes the value.

b. `public static byte option { get; private set; }`

   Calling it outside defaults.option gives the value.

   It's not changeable outside by calling it.

The same is true for functions. Let's explore the same polygon example where two pages (one for area and another for volume) are sharing the same function (Figures 2-6 through 2-9).

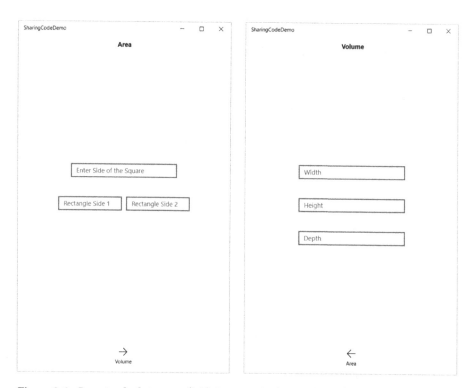

Figure 2-6. *Page 1 calculates area (left), Page 2 calculates volume (right)*

Page 1 XAML

```xml
<Page
    x:Class="SharingCodeDemo.MainPage"
    xmlns="http://schemas.microsoft.com/winfx/2006/xaml/presentation"
    xmlns:x="http://schemas.microsoft.com/winfx/2006/xaml"
    xmlns:local="using:SharingCodeDemo"
    xmlns:d="http://schemas.microsoft.com/expression/blend/2008"
    xmlns:mc="http://schemas.openxmlformats.org/markup-compatibility/2006"
    mc:Ignorable="d">

    <Grid Background="{ThemeResource ApplicationPageBackgroundThemeBrush}">
        <TextBlock x:Name="textBlock" HorizontalAlignment="Center"
        Margin="0,10,0,0" TextWrapping="Wrap" Text="Area"
        VerticalAlignment="Top" FontWeight="Bold"/>
        <TextBox x:Name="squareSide" TextChanged="squareSide_
        TextChanged" Margin="20,0,20,150" TextWrapping="Wrap" Text=""
        VerticalAlignment="Center" PlaceholderText="Enter Side of
        the Square" InputScope="Number" HorizontalAlignment="Center"
        Width="250"/>
        <TextBox x:Name="rectangleSide1" TextChanged="rectangle_TextChanged"
        HorizontalAlignment="Center" Margin="0,0,160,0" TextWrapping="Wrap"
        Text="" VerticalAlignment="Center" Width="150" InputScope="Number"
        PlaceholderText="Rectangle Side 1"/>
        <TextBox x:Name="rectangleSide2" TextChanged="rectangle_TextChanged"
        HorizontalAlignment="Center" Margin="160,0,0,0" TextWrapping="Wrap"
        Text="" VerticalAlignment="Center" Width="150" InputScope="Number"
        PlaceholderText="Rectangle Side 2"/>
        <TextBlock x:Name="polygonArea" HorizontalAlignment="Center"
        Margin="0,0,0,150" TextWrapping="Wrap" Text=""
        VerticalAlignment="Bottom"/>
        <AppBarButton x:Name="volumePageButton" Click="volumePageButton_
        Click" Icon="Forward" Label="Volume" Margin="0,0,0,10"
        VerticalAlignment="Bottom" d:LayoutOverrides="Width"
        HorizontalAlignment="Center"/>

    </Grid>
</Page>
```

Page 1 C#

```csharp
using System;
using Windows.UI.Xaml;
using Windows.UI.Xaml.Controls;
using SharingCodeDemo.sharedArea;
namespace SharingCodeDemo
{
    public sealed partial class MainPage : Page
```

```csharp
{
    public MainPage()
    {
        this.InitializeComponent();
    }

    private void squareSide_TextChanged(object sender,
    TextChangedEventArgs e)
    {
        try
        {
            string sideS = squareSide.Text;
            if(sideS.Length >= 1)
            {
                int side = Convert.ToInt32(sideS);
                double area = sharedFunction.polygon(side);
                polygonArea.Text = "Area of Square = " + area.ToString();
            }
        }
        catch
        {
            polygonArea.Text = "Side of a square must be a numberical
            value";
        }
    }

    private void rectangle_TextChanged(object sender, TextChanged
    EventArgs e)
    {
        try
        {
            string rectS1 = rectangleSide1.Text;
            string rectS2 = rectangleSide2.Text;
            if (rectS1.Length >= 1 && rectS2.Length >= 1)
            {
                int side1 = Convert.ToInt32(rectS1);
                int side2 = Convert.ToInt32(rectS2);
                double area = sharedFunction.polygon(side1, side2);
                polygonArea.Text = "Area of Rectangle = " + area.
                ToString();
            }
        }
        catch
        {
            polygonArea.Text = "Sides of a rectangle must be numberical
            value";
        }
    }
```

```csharp
        private void volumePageButton_Click(object sender, RoutedEventArgs e)
        {
            this.Frame.Navigate(typeof(Page2), null); //Navigation
        }
    }
}
```

Page 2 XAML

```xml
<Page
    x:Class="SharingCodeDemo.Page2"
    xmlns="http://schemas.microsoft.com/winfx/2006/xaml/presentation"
    xmlns:x="http://schemas.microsoft.com/winfx/2006/xaml"
    xmlns:local="using:SharingCodeDemo"
    xmlns:d="http://schemas.microsoft.com/expression/blend/2008"
    xmlns:mc="http://schemas.openxmlformats.org/markup-compatibility/2006"
    mc:Ignorable="d">

    <Grid Background="{ThemeResource ApplicationPageBackgroundThemeBrush}">
        <TextBlock x:Name="textBlock" Margin="0,10,0,0" TextWrapping="Wrap"
        Text="Volume" VerticalAlignment="Top" d:LayoutOverrides="Width"
        HorizontalAlignment="Center" FontWeight="Bold"/>
        <TextBox x:Name="width" TextChanged="box_TextChanged"
        HorizontalAlignment="Center" Margin="0,0,0,150" TextWrapping="Wrap"
        Text="" VerticalAlignment="Center" PlaceholderText="Width"
        Width="250"/>
        <TextBox x:Name="height" TextChanged="box_TextChanged"
        HorizontalAlignment="Center" Margin="0" TextWrapping="Wrap" Text=""
        VerticalAlignment="Center" PlaceholderText="Height" Width="250"/>
        <TextBox x:Name="depth" TextChanged="box_TextChanged"
        HorizontalAlignment="Center" Margin="0,150,0,0" TextWrapping="Wrap"
        Text="" VerticalAlignment="Center" PlaceholderText="Depth"
        Width="250"/>
        <TextBlock x:Name="polygonVolume" Margin="0,0,0,150"
        TextWrapping="Wrap" Text="" VerticalAlignment="Bottom"
        d:LayoutOverrides="Width" HorizontalAlignment="Center"/>
        <AppBarButton x:Name="areaPageButton" Click="areaPageButton_
        Click" Icon="Back" Label="Area" Margin="0,0,0,10"
        VerticalAlignment="Bottom" d:LayoutOverrides="Width"
        HorizontalAlignment="Center"/>
    </Grid>
</Page>
```

Page 2 C#

```csharp
using System;
using Windows.UI.Xaml;
using Windows.UI.Xaml.Controls;
```

```
using SharingCodeDemo.sharedArea;
namespace SharingCodeDemo
{
    public sealed partial class Page2 : Page
    {
        public Page2()
        {
            this.InitializeComponent();
        }
        private void box_TextChanged(object sender, TextChangedEventArgs e)
        {
            try
            {
                string w = width.Text;
                string h = height.Text;
                string d = depth.Text;
                if(w.Length >= 1 && h.Length >=1 && d.Length >= 1)
                {
                    int width = Convert.ToInt32(w);
                    int height = Convert.ToInt32(h);
                    int depth = Convert.ToInt32(d);
                    double volume = sharedFunction.polygon(width, height,
                    depth);
                    polygonVolume.Text = "Volume of Box = " + volume.
                    ToString();
                }
            }
            catch
            {
                polygonVolume.Text = "Please check the inputs provided";
            }
        }

        private void areaPageButton_Click(object sender, RoutedEventArgs e)
        {
            this.Frame.Navigate(typeof(MainPage), null);//Navigation
        }
    }
}
```

Shared Code

```
namespace SharingCodeDemo.sharedArea
{
    class sharedFunction
    {
        public static double polygon(params int[] dimentions)
        {
```

```
            int len = dimentions.Length;
            return len == 1 ? dimentions[0] * dimentions[0] : len == 2 ?
            dimentions[0] * dimentions[1] : len == 3 ? dimentions[0] *
            dimentions[1] * dimentions[2] : -1;
        }
    }
}
```

Figure 2-7. *Area output of Figure 2-6 application*

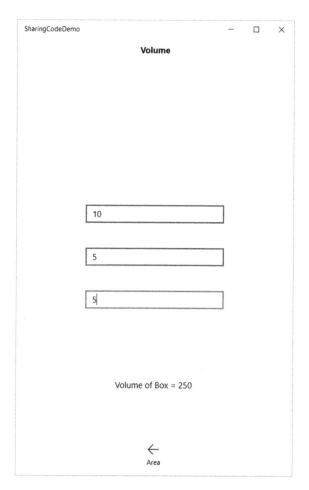

Figure 2-8. *Volume output of Figure 2-6 application*

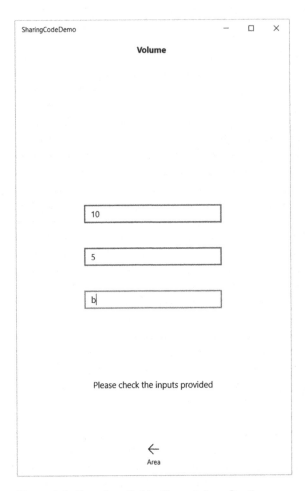

Figure 2-9. Error handled in Figure 2-6 application

Errors and Error Handling

Let's say you have purchased a brand new apartment and along with it you have also purchased insurance on it for protection. You are happy and in peace knowing that you are secure due to that insurance. You are out of town and there's been an earthquake, shattering parts of your apartment. When you go to claim your insurance, the insurance company denies it. Now you read your claim carefully, and you notice a part of the terms that you missed initially stating that you cannot claim insurance if it is due to an act of God (natural disasters).

This section is to prepare you for unexplained or unprecedented incidents. In a computer program, errors can happen a lot of ways. The following examples show some of the ways.

Error Example 1: Due to variables.

```
int a;
int b = a + 10;
```

Here, variable a has not been given a value.

Error Example 2: Due to arrays

```
int[] a = new int[10];
a[10] = 3;
```

Here, the programmer is trying to access the 11th element of the array. If you recall, arrays start from 0 and end in n-1 (n being the number of elements in an array). These types of errors are platform-specific. For example, in MATLAB (Matrix Laboratory) Application arrays start from 1 to n.

Such errors can be avoided by using error prevention methods. Using try catch and throws can do the job. Try catch is more widely used, as the developer (you) has the option to continue running the program and handle the issue internally. The standard statement of the block is

```
try
{
        Body where an exception might occur
}
catch(exception type)
{
    .   What to do when an exception of that type occur
}
finally
{
        Option part. Continue irrespective on an exception.
}
```

Note that the catch and the finally block in a try-catch are completely optional parameters. You use them only if you wish to do something about the errors that occurred. The following is an example of a try-catch block while performing addition:

```
int add = 0;
try
{
        add += number;
}
catch(exception e)
{
        Console.WriteLine("Number was not a valid integer");
}
```

Parallel Programing

Parallel programing (Figure 2-10) can be used when you have a large and complex application. What this does is create multiple threads where each thread does a task.

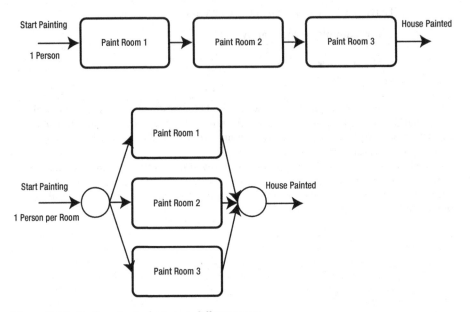

Figure 2-10. *Performing tasks in two different ways*

To demonstrate such a thing, let's look at `Parallel.For`, which is similar to a for loop but runs in parallel in a console application.

```
string[] data = { "Aa", "Bb", "Cc", "Dd", "Ee", "Ff", "Gg", "Hh", "Ii",
"Jj", "Kk", "Ll", "Mm", "Nn" };
int length = data.Length;
for(int i = 0; i < length; i++)
{
        Console.WriteLine(data[i]);
}
```

The same for loop can be rewritten for Parallel.For as

```
Parallel.For(0, length, (i) =>
{
        Console.WriteLine(data[i]);
});
```

You will normally use parallel programming if the order of a computation is not relevant to the outcome. Addition and multiplication are basic examples as result of A + B = B + A and the result of A * B = B * A. More complex parallel computations are used in areas such as rendering of an animated scene or a movie. While parallel programming on CPU is encouraged wherever possible, doing the same thing on a GPU increases the performance of a complex application by a large factor. Since GPU programming in the scope of this book and I do not think it is wise for you to jump straight into such complexities this early but when you have finished this book completely and grasped the concepts well, I'd recommend that you take baby steps into GPU programming by looking at Alea GPU (aleagpu.com). Alea has taken most of the responsibility and headache out of your hands making use of NVIDIA CUDA architecture and presented them in simple C# syntax for you to use the power of a GPU.

While building intelligent programs, you will come across something called *machine learning*. Machine learning can be supervised or unsupervised. Supervised learning is when we have some previous data to work with, and unsupervised learning is somewhat made up as we go along.

We know that human beings are intelligent and we have a learning process. To clarify this, let's consider a classroom with both children and adults in the same room. The lecturer in the classroom asks a simple mathematical question: Is 5 divisible by 2? The children and a few adults immediately respond "No. 5 is not divisible by 2," which is correct according to the level of their learning. But there were some adults who answer "Yes. 5/2 is 2.5" to the query, which is even more accurate. While none of them answered incorrectly, it just means that the children were not introduced to the concept of decimals. Similarly, machine learning grows in its accuracy with more and more data. We shall look more deeply into these concepts in a later chapter.

EXERCISES

Exercise 1: Keeping the thoughts of machine learning in mind, do you think an unmanned helicopter is more stable flying upside down than straight up in both normal and harsh weather conditions? (Remember, it's unmanned so you don't need to consider a human pilot to sit up straight.)

Exercise 2: A standard for loop statement look like

```
for( i, ii, iii)
{
            iv
}
```

where i is the initializer, ii is the condition, iii is the iterator, and iv is the body.

Keeping this in mind, state the order in which they are executed:

a. i, ii, iv, iii

b. i, iv, iii, ii

    c.   i, ii, iii, iv

    d.   None of the above

Exercise 3: Write a loop to summarize the work of Santa Claus delivering Christmas presents every year (in detail).

Exercise 4: Plot a graph to demonstrate the difference in execution time between if-else and switch for

    a.   2 conditions

    b.   5 conditions

    c.   10 conditions

    d.   20 conditions

Exercise 5: Plot a graph to demonstrate the difference in execution time between for and Parallel. For when you try to add

    a.   5 numbers

    b.   50 numbers

    c.   500 numbers

    d.   5,000 numbers

CHAPTER 3

▓ ▓ ▓

The Windows 10 Experience

Every product and every brand is an individual. You may be confused by this statement at first. Just like a person, brands and products do have qualities as a whole. They have qualities, an appearance, and even ideal people for whom the products are built.

When you start building a completely new application or product, you should list your ideal consumer first. There is a distinct difference between a customer and consumer; a customer pays for the product and a consumer uses the product. They can be the same or different individuals. For example, when a dad buys a toy for his kid, the dad becomes the customer and the kid is the consumer. You, as an entrepreneur or a developer, need to know who your customers and consumers are.

After you have made your list, jot down some of the qualities and behaviors of your ideal consumer, such as age group, the movies the person likes, the music the person listens to, and so on.

▓ **Tip**   Always know for whom you are building. List your ideal customer before you start building.

Every cool product boils down to some form of data upon which you can perform basic mathematics. We shall explore this idea in detail in this section and the next chapter. But first let's examine the animation industry and the differences between 2D and 3D productions. Our displays (television, monitor, etc.) have a 2D screen with some width and height. Therefore, if a game developer is building for 2D, the data that the person needs to input are values of width and height.

When 3D was first introduced to the commercial market with 3D movies and games, the output devices still remained 2D. It's not like a user reached his hand into the monitor, making a hole and breaking all the circuits along the way to get something in 3D. Yes, the scenes and models and all the development was in 3D but ultimately the output had to be rendered in 2D.

▓ **Tip**   If unfamiliar with mathematics, make an effort to learn it. It helps in the long run.

Electronic supplementary material The online version of this chapter (doi:10.1007/978-1-4842-2629-2_3) contains supplementary material, which is available to authorized users.

© Ayan Chatterjee 2017
A. Chatterjee, *Building Apps for the Universal Windows Platform*,
DOI 10.1007/978-1-4842-2629-2_3

Figure 3-1 (see color image in source code file) shows a photograph taken in Oxford, England. It has the spatial dimensions of a height of 1500 pixels and a width of 2250 pixels. I am going to perform some operations on it. Figures 3-2 through 3-4 show the RGB layers of the image individually extracted.

Figure 3-1. *Oxford, England*

Figure 3-2. *Red channel of Figure 3-1*

Figure 3-3. *Green channel of Figure 3-1*

Figure 3-4. *Blue channel of Figure 3-1*

With this information, you can do the same custom-defined operations that a professional image manipulation software performs. For practice, let's perform an inversion operation. A single pixel's information in any single band is represented by an unsigned 8-bit integer with a value ranging between 0 and 255. So, to perform inversion, you only need to subtract as follows

Inverted value = 255 – Current Value

The output is displayed in Figure 3-5 (see color image in source code file). For the next example, let's make the image into two colors in each individual channel. The mathematics performed on each of the channels of RGB is as follows

If (Current Value <= 127)

Modified Value = 0

Else

Modified Value = 255

The output of this is displayed in Figure 3-6 (see color image in source code file).

Figure 3-5. *Inversion operation performed on Figure 3-1*

Figure 3-6. *Image converted to two values in individual RGB channels*

So, if you analyze Table 3-1, the total number of possible color combinations in the image is 8 for mathematics wizards.

Table 3-1. *Possible Colors in Figure 3-6*

R	G	B
0	0	0
0	0	255
0	255	0
0	255	255
255	0	0
255	0	255
255	255	0
255	255	255

If you have understood everything to this point, you now know how image filters are created within simple applications to allow users to manipulate selfies as in a professional photo editing application. But if you still have difficulty understanding, let's take another look at the concept. Figure 3-7 provides a summary of an RGB image file.

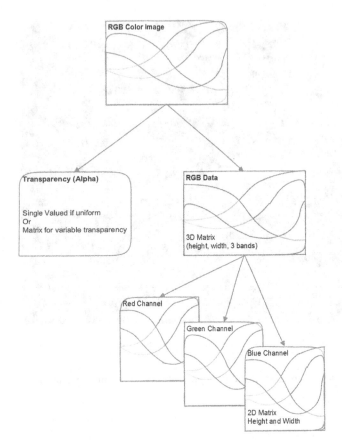

Figure 3-7. *Summary of an RGB color image file*

If you have difficulty understanding this, imagine a rather simplistic example of something you see daily, like a layer of pancakes stacked on top of each other. Every single pancake contains the image information of a particular wavelength. Our human eye can only see pancakes with a wavelength between 400 and 700nm (visible spectrum), the 400nm wavelength being violet and the 700nm wavelength being red. For RGB image information, your camera picks out three pancakes from this visible region: information in wavelengths within red, green, and blue. If your image consists of one single pancake (one band), it is a grayscale image; if your image has three pancakes (three bands in RGB wavelength) it is a color image; if your image has 10 pancake layers (tens of bands), it is called a multispectral image; hundreds of pancakes are a hyperspectral image; and thousands of pancakes are called a ultraspectral image. How many wavelengths and which wavelength information you need depends on what you want to do.

Cortana

Before talking about Cortana, let's take a step back. The very early version of human-computer interaction was through DOS commands (similar to typing commands on command prompt or Windows PowerShell if you have seen or used either). Then human-computer interaction shifted to a GUI (graphical user interface) via the keyboard and mouse. That branched out to touch. Every growth in human-computer level is an attempt to navigate and use the OS (operating system) more completely without the constraint of the previous level. In other words, you can completely use touch to use Windows 10 without the need for a keyboard and mouse.

Cortana is hands-free experience and an attempt to use Windows completely using voice without the need for any other form of interaction. Presently it is in nascent stage and will continue to mature. Previously, with the Windows 8 family, integrating Cortana into your application was done through VCD (voice command definition). VCD is an XML format of data storing information for use in Cortana. A VCD contains the following:

- **Voice commands**

  The root of the XML document containing definitions and schema

- **Command set**

  The parent of a group of commands for a particular language such as US English, UK English, Hindi, French, Mexican, etc.

- **Child elements**

  Such as Command, Listen For, PhraseList, PhraseTopic, etc. to indicate what to listen for (trigger words/phrases) and what happens when the user says one

After defining a VCD, you need to register it to the system when a user first launches the application. This lets Cortana know the trigger words for your application and what happens when a user says one. If VCD doesn't register, Cortana will not get the information to look for and your application will not work with Cortana, as demonstrated in Figure 3-8. To install/register, you declare it during the initialization of the application (inside the Appp.xaml.cs file for a C# project). Let's explore it further with an example. The output is shown in Figure 3-8.

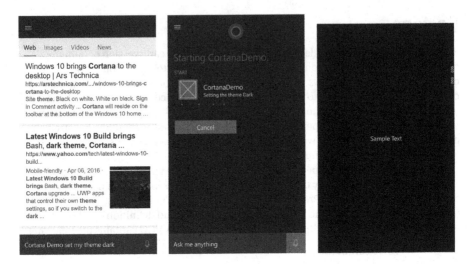

Figure 3-8. *Using voice commands in an example. Cortana fails to respond if VCD is not registered and performs a web search (left), Cortana responds to voice commands if VCD is registered successfully (middle), and Cortana responds to the voice command and turns the application theme dark (right).*

VCD.xml

```xml
<?xml version="1.0" encoding="utf-8" ?>
<VoiceCommands xmlns="http://schemas.microsoft.com/voicecommands/1.2">

  <CommandSet xml:lang="en-us" Name="CortanaDemoVCD_US">
    <AppName> Cortana Demo </AppName>
    <Example> Set App Theme </Example>
    <Command Name="setAppTheme">
      <Example> Setting the application theme </Example>
      <ListenFor RequireAppName="BeforeOrAfterPhrase"> Set [my] theme
      {colors}</ListenFor>
      <ListenFor RequireAppName="ExplicitlySpecified"> Assign
      {builtin:AppName} {colors} </ListenFor>
      <Feedback> Setting the theme {colors} </Feedback>
      <Navigate />
    </Command>
    <PhraseList Label="colors">
      <Item>Light</Item>
      <Item>Dark</Item>
    </PhraseList>
  </CommandSet>

  <CommandSet xml:lang="en-gb" Name="CortanaDemoVCD_UK">
    <AppName> Cortana Demo </AppName>
```

```xml
      <Example> Set App Theme </Example>
      <Command Name="setAppTheme">
        <Example> Repeat what you've just said </Example>
        <ListenFor RequireAppName="BeforeOrAfterPhrase"> Set [my] theme
        {colors}</ListenFor>
        <ListenFor RequireAppName="ExplicitlySpecified"> Assign
        {builtin:AppName} {colors} </ListenFor>
        <Feedback> Setting the theme {colors} </Feedback>
        <Navigate/>
      </Command>
      <PhraseList Label="colors">
        <Item>Light</Item>
        <Item>Dark</Item>
      </PhraseList>

   </CommandSet>
</VoiceCommands>
```

App.xaml.cs

```csharp
using System;
using Windows.ApplicationModel;
using Windows.ApplicationModel.Activation;
using Windows.UI.Xaml;
using Windows.UI.Xaml.Controls;
using Windows.UI.Xaml.Navigation;
using Windows.Storage;
namespace CortanaDemo
{
    sealed partial class App : Application
    {
        public App()
        {
            this.InitializeComponent();
            this.Suspending += OnSuspending;
        }
        protected override async void OnLaunched(LaunchActivatedEventArgs e)
        {
#if DEBUG
            if (System.Diagnostics.Debugger.IsAttached)
            {
                this.DebugSettings.EnableFrameRateCounter = true;
            }
#endif
            Frame rootFrame = Window.Current.Content as Frame;
            if (rootFrame == null)
            {
                rootFrame = new Frame();
```

```
            rootFrame.NavigationFailed += OnNavigationFailed;

            if (e.PreviousExecutionState == ApplicationExecutionState.
            Terminated)
            {
                //TODO: Load state from previously suspended application
            }
            Window.Current.Content = rootFrame;
        }

        if (e.PrelaunchActivated == false)
        {
            if (rootFrame.Content == null)
            {
                rootFrame.Navigate(typeof(MainPage), e.Arguments);
            }
            Window.Current.Activate();
            try
            {
                StorageFile vcdStorageFile = await Package.Current.
                InstalledLocation.GetFileAsync(@"VCD.xml");
                await Windows.ApplicationModel.VoiceCommands.
                VoiceCommandDefinitionManager.InstallCommandDefinitions
                FromStorageFileAsync(vcdStorageFile);
            }
            catch (Exception ex)
            {
                System.Diagnostics.Debug.WriteLine("Installing VCD
                Failed: " + ex.ToString());
            }
        }
    }

    protected override void OnActivated(IActivatedEventArgs args)
    {
        base.OnActivated(args);
        Frame rootFrame = Window.Current.Content as Frame;
        if (rootFrame == null)
        {
            rootFrame = new Frame();
            rootFrame.NavigationFailed += OnNavigationFailed;
            Window.Current.Content = rootFrame;
        }
        if (args.Kind == ActivationKind.VoiceCommand)
        {
            var commandArgs = args as VoiceCommandActivatedEventArgs;
            Windows.Media.SpeechRecognition.SpeechRecognitionResult
            speechRecognitionResult = commandArgs.Result;
```

```
string textSpoken = speechRecognitionResult.Text;
if (textSpoken.Contains("light") || textSpoken.
Contains("Light"))
{
    rootFrame.RequestedTheme = ElementTheme.Light;
}
if(textSpoken.Contains("dark") || textSpoken.
Contains("Dark"))
{
    rootFrame.RequestedTheme = ElementTheme.Dark;
}
}
//Starting the app
rootFrame.Navigate(typeof(MainPage));
Window.Current.Activate();
}

void OnNavigationFailed(object sender, NavigationFailedEventArgs e)
{
    throw new Exception("Failed to load Page " + e.SourcePageType.
    FullName);
}
private void OnSuspending(object sender, SuspendingEventArgs e)
{
    var deferral = e.SuspendingOperation.GetDeferral();
    deferral.Complete();
}
}
}
```

Now that you know how to implement voice commands and use Cortana in your native application, let's take a deeper dive. I started with the statement that Cortana is an attempt to use and navigate an OS with speech, meaning voice commands are your primary medium to communicate with the OS and it is not mandatory for all Cortana-supported devices to have a display. The devices can range from native desktop to Windows Mobile to other mobile devices like iOS and Android to IoT devices to independent Cortana-powered speakers with no display at all. In the previous example, you had the luxury of keeping your business logic embedded within your native application but now, in order to support all of these non-native devices, your business logic needs to move to the cloud; to be more specific, I am talking about bots. The common steps to follow to create and deploy a Cortana skill are the following:

1. Develop your application using the Microsoft Bot Framework (https://dev.botframework.com/).

2. Use the Language Understanding Intelligent Service (LUIS.ai) in your bot to create a natural understanding and intent of what the user wishes to convey.

3. Add speech to your bot.

4. Deploy your bot application to Microsoft Azure using the Azure Publishing Wizard in Visual Studio.

5. The wizard returns deployed details like a destination URL.

6. Register your bot with the Bot Framework (shown in Figure 3-9).

7. Register your registered bot with Cortana skill.

8. Publish your Cortana skill (shown in Figure 3-10).

Figure 3-9. Registering a bot application

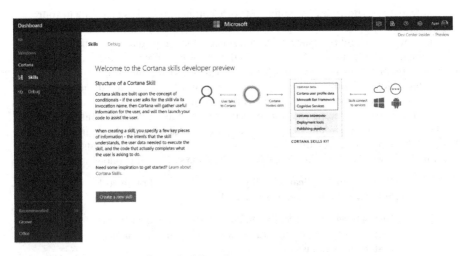

Figure 3-10. Cortana Developer dashboard

That was a brief overview of using Cortana skills to enable your bot on different Cortana supported devices. Since this book is targeted to beginners and beginners migrating to an intermediate level and it's designed to offer a firm grasp of the concepts, it is more important for you to comprehend the core components and features in UWP. Then all of this will flow naturally. I recommend completing all the chapters of this book before taking a deeper dive into the documentation laid out in the Cortana Dev Center (https://docs.microsoft.com/en-us/cortana/getstarted).

Live Tiles

Live tiles (Figure 3-11) are the signature of Windows metro UIs since Windows 8. These are meant to inform a user of an activity within an app without opening the app. It is kind of a summary, much similar to the peek you get when you search with Bing or open your mail application. A few lines of summary show you what to expect.

Some good uses of a live tile implementation are to let the user stay up to date with the current game progress, virtual game coins, a news alert, new unread message, an upcoming event, and so on.

Figure 3-11. Examples of live tiles: weather, news, and store tiles

The Windows 8 family introduced live tiles with some predefined layouts. The next section explores this further.

Notifications

Now that we have discussed live tiles, let's look at other forms that pass information. The whole purpose is to classify the relevance of information. What I mean is, if you were building an email application then you would divide it into something similar to Table 3-2.

Table 3-2. *Types and Recommendations for UWP Notifications*

Notification	Important mail such as from
	• An immediate supervisor at an office
	• A teacher/professor at a university
	• Family (parents, partner, children)
	• Close friends
Live Tile	Relevant yet less important
	• Email from work
	• Email from school (circulation)
	• Email from friends, relatives, and neighbors
	• Total unread email count

An individual uses several types of devices every day, such as a desktop, laptop, tablet, watch, and there are many new and hybrid categories. All of them have a unique notification behavior to maintain. I'll explain this with two hypothetical situations: one where devices followed their own path and the other where the devices have an effective learning algorithm and are synchronized together.

For example, it is raining outside and a person (say Greg) is walking home from work wearing a smartwatch. He also has a phone in his pocket. He is a music fan and has his headphones on. During his walk, one of his colleagues gives him a call. For the first situation, both his watch and his phone ring and vibrate. At the same time, Cortana makes a voice response. It's a nightmare of too many alerts.

Now let's examine the second situation. Greg's phone is already aware of the person making the phone call. Through a learning algorithm, the colleague is not categorized as urgent. So, only a small vibration goes to his watch. His music is not interrupted and his phone does not make any sort of response to disturb Greg in the rain. A risk of water damage to his phone is avoided. Greg can them lift his arm and accept/reject the call right from his wrist.

In UWP, the types of notifications are

- Tile notification

- Toast notification

Tile Notifications

Tile notifications are notifications that update on the application's live tile. The tile sizes available in Windows 10 are small where you only see the application icon; medium, wide, and large tiles are the ones where you are able to update your tile.

Toast Notifications

Toast notifications are the ones peeking from the side for the desktop and peeking in from the top in mobile devices for a while, and they show up on the Action Center.

You will now create a tile and a toast notification. To do that, you will first install the NuGet package shown in Figure 3-12.

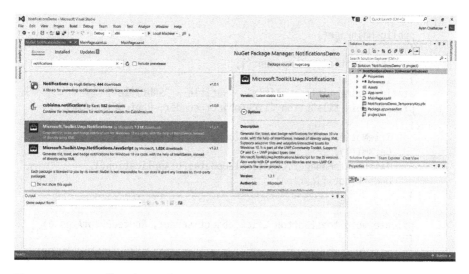

Figure 3-12. *Installing the notification NuGet package*

XAML

```
<Page
    x:Class="NotificationsDemo.MainPage"
    xmlns="http://schemas.microsoft.com/winfx/2006/xaml/presentation"
    xmlns:x="http://schemas.microsoft.com/winfx/2006/xaml"
    xmlns:local="using:NotificationsDemo"
    xmlns:d="http://schemas.microsoft.com/expression/blend/2008"
    xmlns:mc="http://schemas.openxmlformats.org/markup-compatibility/2006"
    mc:Ignorable="d">

    <Grid Background="{ThemeResource ApplicationPageBackgroundThemeBrush}">
        <Button x:Name="tileButton" Click="tileButton_Click" Content="Send
        Tile" Margin="0,100,100,0" VerticalAlignment="Center"
        HorizontalAlignment="Center"/>
        <Button x:Name="toastButton" Click="toastButton_Click" Content="Send
        Toast" HorizontalAlignment="Center" Margin="100,100,0,0"
        VerticalAlignment="Center"/>
    </Grid>
</Page>
```

C#

```
using Windows.UI.Xaml;
using Windows.UI.Xaml.Controls;
using Windows.UI.Notifications;
using Microsoft.Toolkit.Uwp.Notifications;
```

```
namespace NotificationsDemo
{
    public sealed partial class MainPage : Page
    {
        public MainPage()
        {
            this.InitializeComponent();
        }
        static string title = "Title", subtitle = "Subtitle";
        private void tileButton_Click(object sender, RoutedEventArgs e)
        {
            TileNotification notification = new TileNotification(content.
            GetXml());
            TileUpdateManager.CreateTileUpdaterForApplication().
            Update(notification);
        }

        private void toastButton_Click(object sender, RoutedEventArgs e)
        {
            ToastNotification toast = new ToastNotification(toastContent.
            GetXml());
            ToastNotificationManager.CreateToastNotifier().Show(toast);
        }

        TileContent content = new TileContent()
        {
            Visual = new TileVisual()
            {
                TileMedium = new TileBinding()
                {
                    Content = new TileBindingContentAdaptive()
                    {
                        Children =
                        {
                            new AdaptiveText()
                            {
                                Text = title,
                            },

                            new AdaptiveText()
                            {
```

```
                        Text = subtitle,
                        HintStyle = AdaptiveTextStyle.CaptionSubtle
                    },
                }
            }
        },
    }
};

ToastContent toastContent = new ToastContent()
{
    Launch = "app-defined-string",

    Visual = new ToastVisual()
    {
        BindingGeneric = new ToastBindingGeneric()
        {
            Children =
            {
                new AdaptiveText()
                {
                    Text = title
                },

                new AdaptiveText()
                {
                    Text = subtitle
                }
            },
        }
    },

    Actions = new ToastActionsCustom()
    {
        Buttons =
        {
            new ToastButton("dismiss", "cancel")
        },
    }
};
    }
}
```

The output is shown in Figures 3-13 and 3-14.

Figure 3-13. *A tile notification*

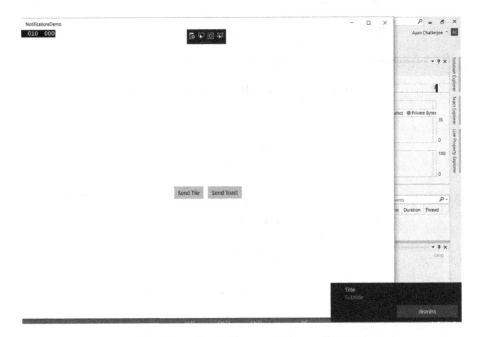

Figure 3-14. *A toast notification*

Settings

If you have a firm grasp of what has been covered, you have come a long way. Now you will take a step further with settings. Let's first analyze the purpose of settings in an application. Settings are for those variables that are unique to an individual. When you were growing up, people used to bomb you with questions like

- What do you want to be when you grow up?

- What is your favorite color?

- When is your birthday?

- What games do you like to play?

- What is your favorite movie?

All these questions were mainly within the process of knowing an individual. For an application, the settings and user preferences you may want to store in an application could be the following

- Color schemes and themes of your application

- User's topics of interest for a news application

- Locations to follow for a weather or tourist application

- Home and work address for a cab service application

- User's favorite places and cuisines preferred for a restaurant search application

- If your application supports multiple pages, store the last page a user was active on before closing it, so the next time they reopen they can pick up where they left off.

You can do this in UWP using local settings and roaming settings. Local settings are settings applicable to the particular system a user sets it in, meaning the settings are applicable on one device only. Roaming settings are those that sync across all of the user's devices a user has signed in using his/her Microsoft Account. Let's explore the concept with an example (Figure 3-15).

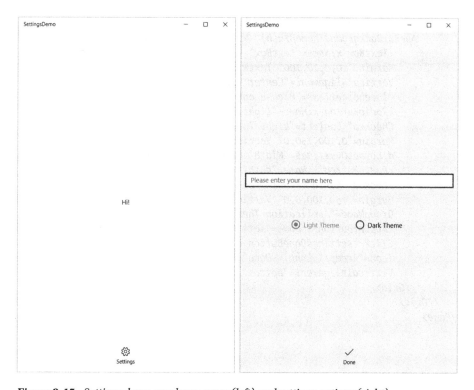

Figure 3-15. *Settings demo app home page (left) and settings options (right)*

Similar to this, you can make your application available in all sorts of color schemes such as light, evening mode, night mode, etc. The XAML and C# for the above example follows:

XAML

```
<Page
    x:Class="SettingsDemo.MainPage"
    xmlns="http://schemas.microsoft.com/winfx/2006/xaml/presentation"
    xmlns:x="http://schemas.microsoft.com/winfx/2006/xaml"
    xmlns:local="using:SettingsDemo"
    xmlns:d="http://schemas.microsoft.com/expression/blend/2008"
    xmlns:mc="http://schemas.openxmlformats.org/markup-compatibility/2006"
    mc:Ignorable="d">

    <Grid x:Name="mainGrid" Background="{ThemeResource
    ApplicationPageBackgroundThemeBrush}" RequestedTheme="Light">
        <TextBlock x:Name="nameText" Margin="0" TextWrapping="Wrap"
        Text="Hi!" VerticalAlignment="Center" d:LayoutOverrides="Width" Hori
        zontalAlignment="Center"/>
        <AppBarButton x:Name="settingsButton" Click="settingsButton_Click"
        HorizontalAlignment="Center" Icon="Setting" Label="Settings"
        Margin="0,0,0,10" VerticalAlignment="Bottom"/>
        <Grid x:Name="settingsGrid" Margin="0" Background="{ThemeResource
        AppBarBackgroundThemeBrush}" Visibility="Collapsed">
            <TextBox x:Name="textBox" TextChanged="textBox_TextChanged"
            Margin="10,0,10,100" TextWrapping="Wrap" Text=""
            VerticalAlignment="Center" d:LayoutOverrides="Width"
            PlaceholderText="Please enter your name here"/>
            <RadioButton x:Name="lightThemeRadio" Checked="lightThemeRadio_
            Checked" Content="Light Theme" HorizontalAlignment="Center"
            Margin="0,100,150,0" VerticalAlignment="Center"
            d:LayoutOverrides="Width" GroupName="Application Theme"/>
            <RadioButton x:Name="darkThemeRadio" Checked="darkThemeRadio_
            Checked" Content="Dark Theme" HorizontalAlignment="Center"
            Margin="150,100,0,0" VerticalAlignment="Center"
            GroupName="Application Theme"/>
            <AppBarButton x:Name="settingsDoneButton"
            Click="settingsDoneButton_Click" HorizontalAlignment="Center"
            Icon="Accept" Label="Done" Margin="0,0,0,10"
            VerticalAlignment="Bottom"/>
        </Grid>
    </Grid>
</Page>
```

C#

```csharp
using Windows.UI.Xaml;
using Windows.UI.Xaml.Controls;
using Windows.Storage;
using Windows.UI.Xaml.Navigation;

namespace SettingsDemo
{
    public sealed partial class MainPage : Page
    {
        string name;
        ApplicationDataContainer local = ApplicationData.Current.
        LocalSettings;
        ApplicationDataContainer roaming = ApplicationData.Current.
        RoamingSettings;

        public MainPage()
        {
            this.InitializeComponent();
        }

        protected override void OnNavigatedTo(NavigationEventArgs e)
        {
            var n = roaming.Values["name"];
            if (n != null)
            {
                name = n.ToString();
                nameText.Text = "Hi! " + name;
                textBox.Text = name;
            }
            var t = local.Values["theme"];
            if(t != null)
            {
                byte theme = System.Convert.ToByte(t.ToString());
                if(theme == 1)
                {
                    lightThemeRadio.IsChecked = true;
                    darkThemeRadio.IsChecked = false;
                    lightThemeRadio.IsEnabled = false;
                    darkThemeRadio.IsEnabled = true;
                    mainGrid.RequestedTheme = ElementTheme.Light;
                }
                else
                {
```

```
                darkThemeRadio.IsChecked = true;
                lightThemeRadio.IsChecked = false;
                darkThemeRadio.IsEnabled = false;
                lightThemeRadio.IsEnabled = true;
                mainGrid.RequestedTheme = ElementTheme.Dark;
            }
        }
        else
        {
            darkThemeRadio.IsChecked = false;
            lightThemeRadio.IsEnabled = false;
            darkThemeRadio.IsEnabled = true;
            mainGrid.RequestedTheme = ElementTheme.Light;
        }
    }

    private void settingsButton_Click(object sender, RoutedEventArgs e)
    {
        settingsGrid.Visibility = Visibility.Visible;
    }

    private void lightThemeRadio_Checked(object sender, RoutedEventArgs e)
    {
        darkThemeRadio.IsChecked = false;
        lightThemeRadio.IsEnabled = false;
        darkThemeRadio.IsEnabled = true;
        mainGrid.RequestedTheme = ElementTheme.Light;
        local.Values["theme"] = 1;
    }

    private void darkThemeRadio_Checked(object sender, RoutedEventArgs e)
    {
        lightThemeRadio.IsChecked = false;
        darkThemeRadio.IsEnabled = false;
        lightThemeRadio.IsEnabled = true;
        mainGrid.RequestedTheme = ElementTheme.Dark;
        local.Values["theme"] = 2;
    }

    private void settingsDoneButton_Click(object sender, RoutedEventArgs e)
    {
        settingsGrid.Visibility = Visibility.Collapsed;
        nameText.Text = "Hi! " + name;
        roaming.Values["name"] = name;
    }
```

```
        private void textBox_TextChanged(object sender, TextChangedEventArgs e)
        {
            name = textBox.Text;
        }
    }
}
```

Share

Sharing data is essential for collaborative creation. Without the sharing of data, your cellular phone call application would not be able to get the phone numbers from your address book application. In UWP, sharing can happen in two ways:

- The actual data is shared

- Address of the application is shared (for large data)

When it's time to share some data, the DataRequested event handler needs to be called. When that happens, the DataRequest object is called, which contains the data to be shared, be it text, URI, or any other type supported in UWP. Figure 3-16 shows the types of data that can be shared and Figure 3-17 shows the output of your demo application.

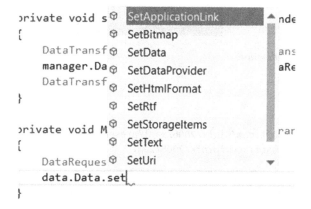

Figure 3-16. *The types of data that can be shared*

69

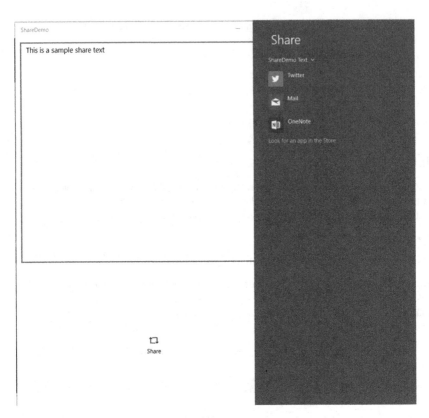

Figure 3-17. *Share charms for the application*

XAML

```
<Page
    x:Class="ShareDemo.MainPage"
    xmlns="http://schemas.microsoft.com/winfx/2006/xaml/presentation"
    xmlns:x="http://schemas.microsoft.com/winfx/2006/xaml"
    xmlns:local="using:ShareDemo"
    xmlns:d="http://schemas.microsoft.com/expression/blend/2008"
    xmlns:mc="http://schemas.openxmlformats.org/markup-compatibility/2006"
    mc:Ignorable="d">
    <Grid Background="{ThemeResource ApplicationPageBackgroundThemeBrush}">
        <TextBox x:Name="textBox" TextChanged="textBox_TextChanged"
        Margin="10,10,10,300" TextWrapping="Wrap" Text=""
        PlaceholderText="type your share text here"/>
        <AppBarButton x:Name="shareButton" Click="shareButton_Click"
        IsEnabled="False" HorizontalAlignment="Center" Icon="ReShare"
        Label="Share" Margin="0,0,0,100" VerticalAlignment="Bottom"
        d:LayoutOverrides="Width"/>
    </Grid>
</Page>
```

C#

```csharp
using Windows.ApplicationModel.DataTransfer;
using Windows.UI.Xaml;
using Windows.UI.Xaml.Controls;

namespace ShareDemo
{
    public sealed partial class MainPage : Page
    {
        public MainPage()
        {
            this.InitializeComponent();
        }

        private void textBox_TextChanged(object sender, TextChangedEventArgs e)
        {
            if(textBox.Text == "")
            {
                shareButton.IsEnabled = false;
            }
            else
            {
                shareButton.IsEnabled = true;
            }
        }

        private void shareButton_Click(object sender, RoutedEventArgs e)
        {
            DataTransferManager manager = DataTransferManager.GetFor
            CurrentView();
            manager.DataRequested += Manager_DataRequested;
            DataTransferManager.ShowShareUI();
        }

        private void Manager_DataRequested(DataTransferManager sender,
        DataRequestedEventArgs args)
        {
            DataRequest data = args.Request;
            data.Data.SetText(textBox.Text);
            data.Data.Properties.Title = "ShareDemo Text";
        }
    }
}
```

Navigation

Coach (Economy Class) passengers in a flight land on the ground the same time as First Class and Business Class passengers. However, the experiences of each are completely different. The Business Class experience is designed for business users, meaning after a 10-hour flight the passenger is expected to land fresh and prepared for the next business meeting. Rather than just navigating from one page to the next, you as a developer can achieve the same kind of first class experience for your users. This can include the following:

- Page navigation animation

- Keeping a flow from one page to the next

- Preloading data like forms and maps

- Offline experience for pages that require Internet access and if the user's Internet connection is slow or offline

- Storing user-typed data whenever required for unavailable network

- Assigning user-friendly correct error messages for different kinds of errors

In a complex application with tons of page hierarchy, you may want to design a navigation first before implementation. Navigation design will allow you to understand the intuitive nature of your app's navigation. It will also let you know if there is any dead end to the navigation structure.

To navigate from one page to the next, `Frame.Navigate` is used. The syntax is as follows:

```
Frame.Navigate(typeof(Page), parameters)
```

It's always a good practice to be prepared for any kind of errors your application might encounter. Similarly, when navigation fails to occur, it's a good practice to use `NavigationFailed`. Let's look at an implementation. The output is shown in Figure 3-18.

Page 1 XAML

```
<Page
    x:Class="NavigationDemo.MainPage"
    xmlns="http://schemas.microsoft.com/winfx/2006/xaml/presentation"
    xmlns:x="http://schemas.microsoft.com/winfx/2006/xaml"
    xmlns:local="using:NavigationDemo"
    xmlns:d="http://schemas.microsoft.com/e xpression/blend/2008"
    xmlns:mc="http://schemas.openxmlformats.org/markup-compatibility/2006"
    mc:Ignorable="d">
```

```
    <Grid Background="{ThemeResource ApplicationPageBackgroundThemeBrush}">
        <TextBlock Text="Page 1" HorizontalAlignment="Center"
        VerticalAlignment="Center" />
        <AppBarButton x:Name="navigateToPage2" Click="navigateToPage2_
        Click" Label="Page 2" Icon="Go" VerticalAlignment="Bottom"
        HorizontalAlignment="Center" Margin="0,0,0,10" />
    </Grid>
</Page>
```

Page 1 C#

```csharp
using Windows.UI.Xaml.Controls;
namespace NavigationDemo
{
    public sealed partial class MainPage : Page
    {
        public MainPage()
        {
            this.InitializeComponent();
        }
        private void navigateToPage2_Click(object sender, Windows.UI.Xaml.
        RoutedEventArgs e)
        {
            Frame.Navigate(typeof(Page2));
        }
    }
}
```

Page 2 XAML

```xml
<Page
    x:Class="NavigationDemo.Page2"
    xmlns="http://schemas.microsoft.com/winfx/2006/xaml/presentation"
    xmlns:x="http://schemas.microsoft.com/winfx/2006/xaml"
    xmlns:local="using:NavigationDemo"
    xmlns:d="http://schemas.microsoft.com/expression/blend/2008"
    xmlns:mc="http://schemas.openxmlformats.org/markup-compatibility/2006"
    mc:Ignorable="d">
    <Grid Background="{ThemeResource ApplicationPageBackgroundThemeBrush}">
        <TextBlock Text="Page 2" HorizontalAlignment="Center"
        VerticalAlignment="Center" />
        <AppBarButton x:Name="backButton" Click="backButton_
        Click" Label="Back" Icon="Back" VerticalAlignment="Top"
        HorizontalAlignment="Left" Margin="0" />
    </Grid>
</Page>
```

Page 2 C#

```csharp
using Windows.UI.Xaml.Controls;
namespace NavigationDemo
{
    public sealed partial class Page2 : Page
    {
        public Page2()
        {
            this.InitializeComponent();
        }
        private void backButton_Click(object sender, Windows.UI.Xaml.Routed
        EventArgs e)
        {
            Frame.Navigate(typeof(MainPage));
        }
    }
}
```

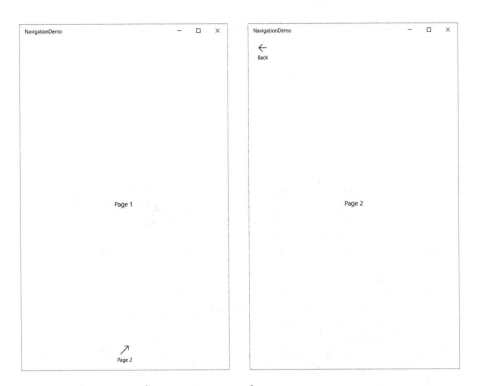

Figure 3-18. *Navigating from one page to another*

In the previous example, we talked about navigating between two different pages within the same window. But sometimes your application may require multiple windows. One good example is Mail, where you can click on a button to open the contents of your email in a new window. You will need to create multiple windows to provide a more dedicated experience to separate contents in your application like a UWP notepad application where each text document is presented in a different window. Let's take a look at an implementation that is the same as the previous one but instead of navigating to the second page, it is going to open a new window for the second page. Some parts of the code may be unfamiliar to you and may confuse you but do not read too much into it. As you proceed, you will get more and more familiar with UWP application development. The output of this application is shown in Figure 3-19.

XAML (Main Page)

```
<Page
    x:Class="MultipleViewDemo.MainPage"
    xmlns="http://schemas.microsoft.com/winfx/2006/xaml/presentation"
    xmlns:x="http://schemas.microsoft.com/winfx/2006/xaml"
    xmlns:local="using:MultipleViewDemo"
    xmlns:d="http://schemas.microsoft.com/expression/blend/2008"
    xmlns:mc="http://schemas.openxmlformats.org/markup-compatibility/2006"
    mc:Ignorable="d">
    <Grid Background="{ThemeResource ApplicationPageBackgroundThemeBrush}">
        <TextBlock HorizontalAlignment="Center" Margin="0,10,0,0"
        TextWrapping="Wrap" Text="Page 1" VerticalAlignment="Top"/>
        <AppBarButton x:Name="page2Button" Click="page2Button_Click"
        HorizontalAlignment="Right" Icon="Go" Label="Page 2" Margin="0"
        VerticalAlignment="Center"/>
    </Grid>
</Page>
```

XAML (Page 2)

```
<Page
    x:Class="MultipleViewDemo.Page2"
    xmlns="http://schemas.microsoft.com/winfx/2006/xaml/presentation"
    xmlns:x="http://schemas.microsoft.com/winfx/2006/xaml"
    xmlns:local="using:MultipleViewDemo"
    xmlns:d="http://schemas.microsoft.com/expression/blend/2008"
    xmlns:mc="http://schemas.openxmlformats.org/markup-compatibility/2006"
    mc:Ignorable="d">
    <Grid Background="{ThemeResource ApplicationPageBackgroundThemeBrush}">
        <TextBlock HorizontalAlignment="Center" Margin="0"
        TextWrapping="Wrap" Text="Page 2" VerticalAlignment="Center"/>
    </Grid>
</Page>
```

C# (Main Page)

```csharp
using System;
using Windows.ApplicationModel.Core;
using Windows.UI.ViewManagement;
using Windows.UI.Xaml;
using Windows.UI.Xaml.Controls;
namespace MultipleViewDemo
{
    public sealed partial class MainPage : Page
    {
        public MainPage()
        {
            this.InitializeComponent();
        }

        private async void page2Button_Click(object sender, RoutedEventArgs e)
        {
            CoreApplicationView page2View = CoreApplication.CreateNewView();
            int page2ViewID = 0;
            await page2View.Dispatcher.RunAsync(Windows.UI.Core.Core
            DispatcherPriority.Normal, () =>
            {
                Frame newFrame = new Frame();
                newFrame.Navigate(typeof(Page2), null);
                Window.Current.Content = newFrame;
                Window.Current.Activate();
                page2ViewID = ApplicationView.GetForCurrentView().Id;
            });
            await ApplicationViewSwitcher.TryShowAsStandaloneAsync
            (page2ViewID);
        }
    }
}
```

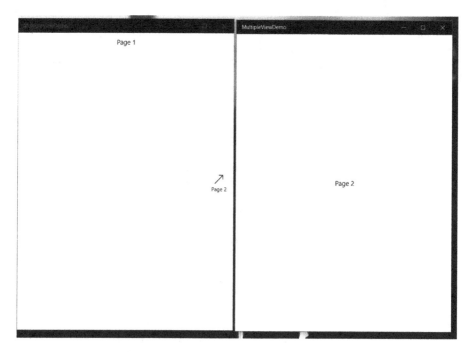

Figure 3-19. *Output of multiple views application*

In-App Purchases (IAPs)

You walk into a fast food restaurant franchise and are looking at the food/drink items offered. Once you have decided what to have, you walk into the counter and tell the person what you want. For instance, let's say you have decided to have chicken fries. The person taking your order asks you if you want the chicken spicy or non-spicy (skillfully omitting the by-default option). These are add-ons to the menu, which will increase your bill total and without realizing you have purchased an add-on. In other words, you have purchased an additional option within the product, which makes it an in-app purchase. But good news here is that with Windows IAPs we have the decency to let a user know of the IAPs and prices before the user makes a purchase. IAPs are either

- Consumable, or
- Durable

Consumable, as the name suggests can be eaten up or consumed (like candy!). It is a one-time thing. An example of a consumable IAP is to purchase virtual currency in a game in the form of game coins. A durable IAP, on the other hand, is an IAP that is purchased and stands true for a certain amount of time, be it days, weeks, months, or forever. An example of this is the purchase of a digital music album.

Subscriptions are continued, durable purchases. To implement IAP in your application, a flow should have already formed in your mind that there must be an API for your application to communicate with Windows Store, each IAP should have their unique ID, and there should be some kind of metadata somewhere describing your IAPs. Taking it step by step,

1. The Windows.Services.Store (Windows.ApplicationModel. Store was the older one until Windows 10 version 1607 but that'll fade away as time goes) namespace is the one that contains all the APIs your mind thought about.

2. Step 2 is to initialize your app's license information. There are two classes to consider: CurrentApp and CurrentAppSimulator. As the name suggests, CurrentAppSimulator is for you to simulate and try out if your IAP implementation is working without actually purchasing anything, and CurrentApp is the real thing to be used to make purchases. The syntax is

   ```
   licenseInformation = CurrentAppSimulator.License
   Information;
   ```

3. Step 3 is defining your IAPs. For CurrentApp to be effective and prior to publication on Windows Store, you need create IAPs for your app in the developer portal and define their metadata there. And for CurrentAppSimulator, if you are testing before publication, you need to create an XML document and call it during execution much like how you did with VCD and Cortana on a local device.

4. Step 4 is to implement those IAP(s) in your application and the regular drill follows: seeing if your IAP is active and all the errors and warnings for failures like connection failures, user initiates but then cancels the IAP purchase, etc.

Example:

```
async void BuyFeature()
{
    if (!licenseInformation.ProductLicenses["IAP1"].IsActive)
    {
        try
        {
            await CurrentApp.RequestProductPurchaseAsync("IAP1", false);
                //do your stuff and check if IAP was successful
        }
        catch (Exception)
        {
```

```
            // Error handling
        }
    }
    else
    {
        // User already owns this feature.
    }
}
```

EXERCISES

Exercise 1: In the previous chapter, the `params` keyword was used in the PolymorphismConsoleDemo application. Explain how it may or may not be correct.

Hint:

```
function main(args)
{
    Function1(argument 1)
    Function1(argument 1, argument 2)
}
```

Is it polymorphism to have two functions named `Function1` or one with `params`? Which one exhibits many forms?

Exercise 2: Build an application implementing a live tile and a toast notification from code behind.

Exercise 3: Try sharing a binary data with another application.

Exercise 4: Explore the following keywords:

a.   Namespace

b.   Enumeration

c.   Structure

d.   GUID

Exercise 5: Learn how to implement skills and make use of Cortana in iOS and Android devices.

CHAPTER 4

■ ■ ■

Windows with Mouse and Keyboard

What falls under basic knowledge and what falls under advanced? In the ancient ages, something like a catapult was considered highly advanced and yet projectile motion is taught today in middle school physics class. So, is it a function of time? Or is it a function of progress and advancement? In this chapter, I will take a bold step and consider development with a mouse and keyboard part of basic knowledge.

In the previous chapter, I talked about how an image is split into RGB channels and how we can perform mathematical operations to create something like image filters. In this chapter, I shall take it a bit further, so you can be prepared to be a part of the next decade of innovation.

If you have studied/are studying high school physics, you should recall that all the colors of a rainbow come out of a white light when passed through a prism: violet to red. An RGB color camera captures information from three wavelengths (one from the red region, one from the green, and a third from the blue wavelength region). A single layer of image in one wavelength is called a band. And you have also studied in high school that there are ultraviolet and infrared regions beyond visible, which we cannot see with our naked eye. It does not mean that we cannot capture data from those wavelengths, however. Special cameras called image spectrometers can capture that data. How do you think the Windows Hello camera can distinguish between your face and a photo of your face? How do you think those heat vision goggles work in real life (you must have seen a ton of them being substituted if you play first-person shooter games)? It is because some of the data is captured from outside the visible region to obtain a conclusion; some may be from absorption wavelengths and some may be from emission wavelengths.

With this information, you can create your own unique IoT (Internet of Things) application. For instance, a lot of organic farmers are actively using it to identify healthy crops from unhealthy ones to stay ahead in the market. A plant with more chlorophyll is found to reflect more NIR (near infrared) energy than an unhealthy plant. Read Chapter 6 for more information on how to create an IoT application.

© Ayan Chatterjee 2017

A. Chatterjee, *Building Apps for the Universal Windows Platform*,
DOI 10.1007/978-1-4842-2629-2_4

■ **Tip** Much like machine learning, all of us are learning every day. Learning is a human nature. So, the algorithms or whatever you learn here are not absolute. It is more important to know how things really work instead of memorizing the steps, and it's most important to learn how you can contribute to make things better.

Components of a Solution

When you first create a new UWP application, you will see some files put in by default, as shown in Figure 4-1. Let's discuss what they are and what they do.

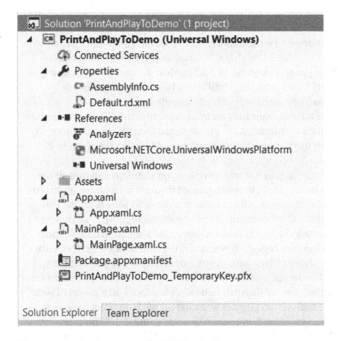

Figure 4-1. Components of a UWP solution

- **Solution**

  An entire collection of projects and build settings

- **Project**

  A single project. Think of a project as one room and a solution as one apartment containing one or even a few rooms

- **Connected Services**

  External and third-party services that can be configured to work with your application like Office 365 API, Azure Cloud Storage, Azure IoT Hub, etc.

- **Properties**

  - **Assembly Information**

    When you build an application, an equivalent executable is created with a version number like 1.0.0.0 (the format is <Major Version>.<Minor Version>.<Build Number>.<Revision>). This file contains this information related to your project.

  - `Default.rd.xml`

    An XML configuration file for your project's runtime directives (rd).

- **References**

  Every connected service, your UWP project, external components, NuGet packages, and even another project you have written can be a reference. A reference is required to implement the containers contained in them.

- **Assets**

  Your application's tile and other images. You do not need to store your images in this folder but it has become a common standard of practice among developers to store in this folder and even create subfolders here if need be.

- **Default Application Class**

  The default application class (`App.xaml` and `App.xaml.cs`) is the first page that is called when your application is launched. This class also initiates the root frame and directs to your main page.

- **Page**

  Your XMAL and its associated C# files where you do your UI design and back-end stuff.

- **Manifest**

  Another XML document but this one contains information about the UWP project like the application and your identity, tiles, device capabilities to be used, etc.

- **Temporary key**

  Your application's certificate file (shown in Figure 4-2) to deploy to your device. It is required for ClickOnce deployment and contains information such as the time stamp of your application.

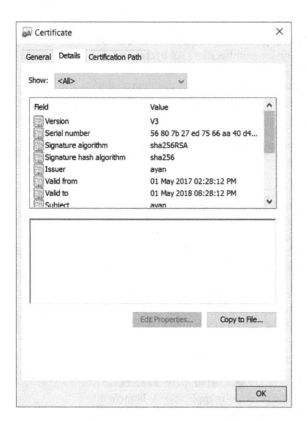

Figure 4-2. *Information stored in the temporary key certificate*

Visual Studio and Blend

Figure 4-3 shows the Visual Studio window divided into three major sections. All of these windows are resizable and can be moved in a drag and drop way.

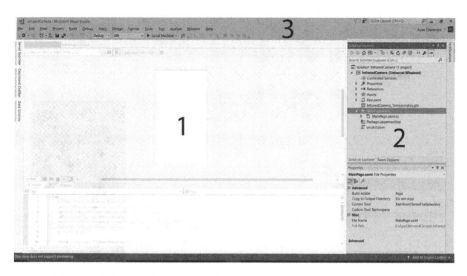

Figure 4-3. *Visual Studio window for a blank UWP project*

To explain the basic layout,

1. The workspace is where you code, build your stuff, open multiple pages in tabs, split the screen between pages, or a build/debug window, etc. Whatever it is that you do or like to do, the workspace is your place to work.

2. The explorer and properties spot is where you browse/view your project and its associated files, all the image files you have in your assets, your team explorer, and any additional information and properties an object may have such as making a button pretty by adding colors and borders.

3. The menu options are where you have the menus, preferences, and settings including build configurations and locations from where all your external tools are called.

We have covered the use of Visual Studio in previous chapters, so let's hop forward to testing your functions with Unit Tests. Unit testing is a piece of code that you write to test individual components of your application. For this example, you will create a simple UWP application to add two numbers and create a unit test for the project. To create a unit test, first create a unit test library or unit test application, as shown in Figure 4-4.

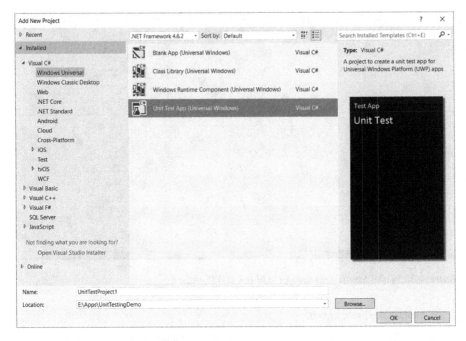

Figure 4-4. Unit test application for UWP

After you have done that, you need to specify the project for which you are creating. In other words, you need to add a reference to the unit test project, as shown in Figure 4-5.

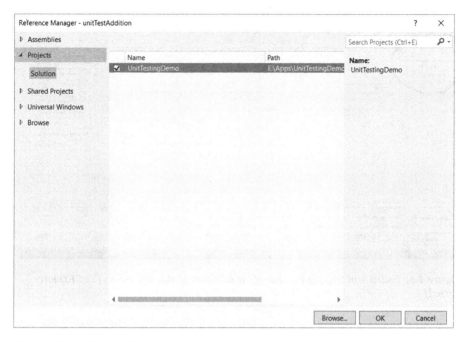

Figure 4-5. *Adding a reference to a unit test project*

When these two steps are done, you can start writing your unit tests. For this demonstration, you shall create one unit test to test if two numbers are being added correctly. For the first run (Figure 4-6), the test fails because of a silly mistake of adding the absolute values of the numbers, and the app will produce incorrect results for negative numbers if you distributed it to the public. When that is corrected, the test runs fine (Figure 4-7). In this way, you can use unit tests to verify parts of your application that may produce incorrect results.

Figure 4-6. *Failed unit tests die because of the addition of absolute values (Test Explorer circled)*

Figure 4-7. *Successful unit test upon fixing the issue*

Visual Studio 2017 introduces live unit testing, which means once you have successfully built your unit tests, you can turn on live unit testing to run the tests as you debug your application.

XAML

```xml
<Page
    x:Class="UnitTestingDemo.MainPage"
    xmlns="http://schemas.microsoft.com/winfx/2006/xaml/presentation"
    xmlns:x="http://schemas.microsoft.com/winfx/2006/xaml"
    xmlns:local="using:UnitTestingDemo"
    xmlns:d="http://schemas.microsoft.com/expression/blend/2008"
    xmlns:mc="http://schemas.openxmlformats.org/markup-compatibility/2006"
    mc:Ignorable="d">
    <Grid Background="{ThemeResource ApplicationPageBackgroundThemeBrush}">
        <AppBarButton x:Name="computeButton" Click="computeButton_Click"
        HorizontalAlignment="Center" Icon="Add" Label="Compute"
        Margin="0,0,0,150" VerticalAlignment="Bottom"/>
        <TextBlock x:Name="result" HorizontalAlignment="Center" Margin="0,0,0,20"
        TextWrapping="Wrap" Text="" VerticalAlignment="Bottom"/>
        <TextBox x:Name="num1" Margin="20,100,20,0" TextWrapping="Wrap"
        Text="" VerticalAlignment="Top" PlaceholderText="Number 1"/>
        <TextBox x:Name="num2" Margin="20,200,20,0" TextWrapping="Wrap"
        Text="" VerticalAlignment="Top" PlaceholderText="Number 2"/>
    </Grid>
</Page>
```

C#

```csharp
using System;
using Windows.UI.Xaml;
using Windows.UI.Xaml.Controls;
namespace UnitTestingDemo
{
    public sealed partial class MainPage : Page
    {
        public MainPage()
        {
            this.InitializeComponent();
        }
        private void computeButton_Click(object sender, RoutedEventArgs e)
        {
            try
            {
                double n1 = Convert.ToDouble(num1.Text);
                double n2 = Convert.ToDouble(num2.Text);
                result.Text = addNumbers(n1, n2).ToString();
            }
            catch { }
        }
```

```
        public static double addNumbers(double n1, double n2)
        {
            return n1 + n2;
        }
    }
}
```

Unit Test C#

```
using System;
using Microsoft.VisualStudio.TestTools.UnitTesting;
namespace unitTestAddition
{
    [TestClass]
    public class UnitTest1
    {
        [TestMethod]
        public void testingAddition()
        {
            double test1Result = UnitTestingDemo.MainPage.addNumbers(-3, 2);
            Assert.AreEqual(-1, test1Result);
        }
    }
}
```

When you click the green run button to debug and test your application, a couple of steps occur. Of course, you can do all of them one at a time using the command line or configure the debugging settings to suit your needs. By default, a couple of options are put in place to make your job easier and so that you can focus on your essential algorithms rather than worrying about libraries and build settings.

Before debugging, you will need to pick the device you wish to test your application on. Note in the figure that the devices are shown using their device name and the version of operating system they are using. The ones in the drop-down menu are the devices recognized by Visual Studio. The ones that do not come up, such as IoT devices, can be put in remote debugging settings.

Designing in Blend

Blend is for a front-end designer who is building the user interface. Blend hides all the code behind "behind" and makes a designer really focus on the UI without worrying about anything else. In this section, I will focus on the user interface aspects and how to design a good UI in Blend.

Figure 4-8 shows the default layout of Blend when you first open a page of your application. Of course, they can be moved around to suit your needs. The following are present in the layout (left to right, as shown in Figure 4-8):

- **Solution Explorer**

  This is where you see the files for your Visual Studio solution.

- **Assets**

  These are the assets (button, text box, etc.) as defined in the schema for the presentation layer.

- **States**

  Visual states of your application

- **Data**

  Data that you may need to work with

- **Objects and timeline**

  The XAML hierarchical structure of your UI

- **Tools**

  These are present between the workspace and the left panel such as the hand tool, pen tool, zoom tool, etc.

- **Workspace of your page**

- **Properties**

  To display the available properties of a selected element

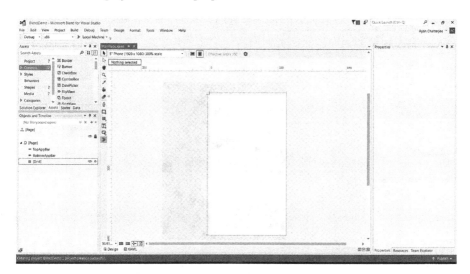

Figure 4-8. *XAML visual designer in Blend for Visual Studio*

To put an element on your page, simply drag and drop it from your assets. Selecting the asset on the workspace will display a list of properties you can modify.

Figure 4-9 shows that four ellipses and a text block were dragged and dropped onto the scene and the color properties of the ellipses were modified. When you move the margins of a grid around, a triangle-shaped object will appear along with a horizontal/vertical line all the way through the grid. You can place them to separate your layout into rows and columns. `RowDefinition` and `ColumnDefinition` are used to define your rows and columns. If you are going to use the visual designer in Blend, you can define your rows/columns and just drag and drop objects. But if you are going to be writing XAML, you need to first define your rows and columns and then place your objects. For example, to create thee rows and place two objects on the first and second row, the XAML is the following:

```
<Grid>
        <Grid.RowDefinitions>
                <RowDefinition Height="100px"/>
                <RowDefinition Height="1*"/>
                <RowDefinition Height="2*"/>
        </Grid.RowDefinitions>
        <SomeObject Grid.Row="0"/>
        <AnotherObject Grid.Row="1"/>
</Grid>
```

In this example, the three rows are given a height of 100 pixels, 1x and 2x, respectively. In other words, if the total height is 500 pixels, the first row gets a fixed 100 pixels, and the remaining 400 pixels are divided by 1x + 2x = 3x or x = 400/3, thus the respective height for the second and third rows are 400/3 and 2*400/3 pixels for that particular display. Later in this chapter, I will go through concepts such as visual states and scalable assets and how you can use them to better design your UWP application.

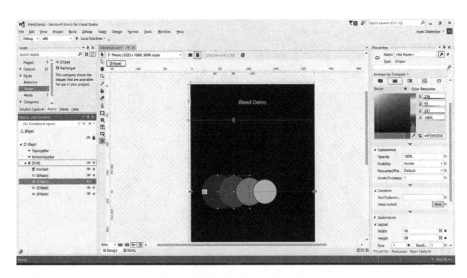

Figure 4-9. *Adding some assets to the page*

If you are used to a professional design software like Adobe Illustrator or Affinity Designer or used to drawing on drawing tablets (like the ones made by Wacom), there is a pen tool available in Blend to draw custom vector shapes, as shown in Figure 4-10.

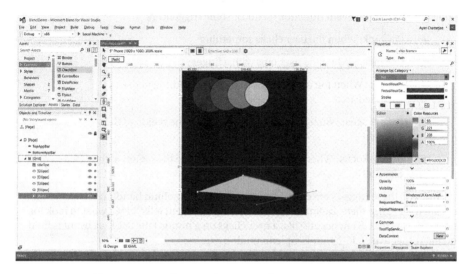

Figure 4-10. *Adding a custom shape with a pen tool*

All of these assets are defined in the schema. If you flip to XAML code, you can see them at the top of your XAML page:

```
<x:Class="CameraDemo.MainPage"
xmlns="http://schemas.microsoft.com/winfx/2006/xaml/presentation"
xmlns:x="http://schemas.microsoft.com/winfx/2006/xaml"
xmlns:local="using:CameraDemo"
xmlns:d="http://schemas.microsoft.com/expression/blend/2008"
xmlns:mc="http://schemas.openxmlformats.org/markup-compatibility/2006"
mc:Ignorable="d">
```

In the first line, `x:Class` is the full qualified name of your class. The second and third lines specify almost all types of assets and their properties. Every element on your page has a name. The property `Name` is defined in line 2 (`xmlns`) whereas the one with `x:Name` is defined in line 3 (`xmlns:x`) of the above header. If you remove the line `xmlns` on line 2, all your buttons and text boxes will give an error because their schema will not be defined.

W3C (World Wide Web Consortium) is an international community and their schemas are used in many business applications worldwide. The appearance and behaviors of your buttons and other elements that you put in your application can't just come out of the blue. They need to be defined somewhere and these `xmlns` namespaces contain the root element and XAML definitions. To define your own custom control, you need to have your own schema, which I will discuss later in this chapter.

93

Triggers and Actions

A *trigger* is the initiation and an *action* is what follows. For instance, when the user presses a button, it is a trigger. Triggers are anything caused by the user of your application to start an event (function/action). Some triggers are

- OnClick: When the user clicks something

- OnTapped: When the user taps with a finger

- OnDrop: When the user drags and drops something in the specified area

- OnGotFocus: When the mouse moves inside the region of the element

- OnLostFocus: When the mouse moves outside the region of the element

In UWP, these triggers are called *events* and the code behind handling those events are called *event handlers*. Defining events in your UIElement tells XAML what to look for, and as soon as that event occurs (like a user clicks on a button) the OnClick event is fired and the respective code-behind implementation executes.

Size Classes/Visual States

I have talked about how Windows 10 is meant to run on all kinds of devices. This also means that you, as a developer, are expected to accommodate different user interface designs depending on the size of a display. If you are migrating from an Apple development environment, you will know them as size classes but in UWP they are known as *visual states*. This lets you specify UI design and UI elements for a particular range of width and height values. You, as a developer, are in control of your application and you can decide how your app should look on different sizes of devices. Let's take a look at an example (Figure 4-11) to implement this concept.

Figure 4-11. *Visual states in Blend*

To create a visual state, just create a visual state group and then the visual states below it. As a developer, you only need to work with adaptive pixels. Figures 4-12, 4-13, and 4-14 show two visual states implemented. Once you have defined a visual state in Blend, you can just click it to make it active and design, resize, rescale, and show/hide some components to make it best for the screen size.

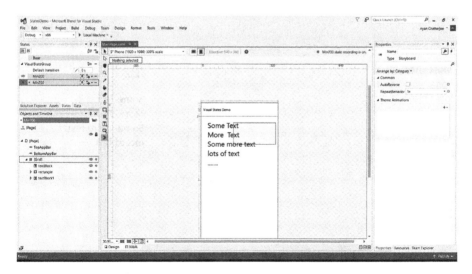

Figure 4-12. *Two visual states implemented*

Figure 4-13. *Adaptive trigger window*

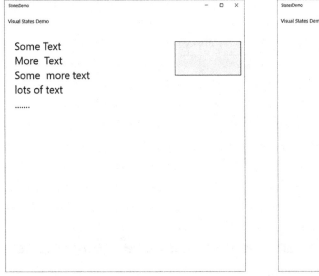

Figure 4-14. *Output of visual states demo application*

XAML

```xml
<Page
    x:Class="StatesDemo.MainPage"
    xmlns="http://schemas.microsoft.com/winfx/2006/xaml/presentation"
    xmlns:x="http://schemas.microsoft.com/winfx/2006/xaml"
    xmlns:local="using:StatesDemo"
    xmlns:d="http://schemas.microsoft.com/expression/blend/2008"
    xmlns:mc="http://schemas.openxmlformats.org/markup-compatibility/2006"
    mc:Ignorable="d">

    <Grid Background="{ThemeResource ApplicationPageBackgroundThemeBrush}">
        <VisualStateManager.VisualStateGroups>
            <VisualStateGroup x:Name="VisualStateGroup">
                <VisualState x:Name="Min200">
                    <VisualState.StateTriggers>
                        <AdaptiveTrigger MinWindowWidth="200"/>
                    </VisualState.StateTriggers>
                </VisualState>
                <VisualState x:Name="Min700">
                    <VisualState.Setters>
                        <Setter Target="textBlock1.(FrameworkElement.Margin)">
                            <Setter.Value>
                                <Thickness>30,20,0,0</Thickness>
                            </Setter.Value>
                        </Setter>
                        <Setter Target="textBlock1.(FrameworkElement.
                        HorizontalAlignment)" Value="Left"/>
                        <Setter Target="rectangle.(FrameworkElement.Margin)">
                            <Setter.Value>
                                <Thickness>0,30,10,0</Thickness>
                            </Setter.Value>
                        </Setter>
                        <Setter Target="rectangle.(FrameworkElement.
                        HorizontalAlignment)" Value="Right"/>
                    </VisualState.Setters>
                    <VisualState.StateTriggers>
                        <AdaptiveTrigger MinWindowWidth="700"/>
                    </VisualState.StateTriggers>
                </VisualState>
            </VisualStateGroup>
        </VisualStateManager.VisualStateGroups>
        <Grid.RowDefinitions>
            <RowDefinition Height="60"/>
            <RowDefinition/>
        </Grid.RowDefinitions>
```

```xml
    <TextBlock x:Name="textBlock" HorizontalAlignment="Left"
    Margin="10,0,0,0" TextWrapping="Wrap" Text="Visual States Demo"
    VerticalAlignment="Center"/>
    <Rectangle x:Name="rectangle" Fill="#FFF4F4F5"
    Height="100" Margin="0,10,0,0" Grid.Row="1" Stroke="Black"
    VerticalAlignment="Top" Width="200"/>
    <TextBlock x:Name="textBlock1" HorizontalAlignment="Center"
    Margin="0,150,0,0" Grid.Row="1" TextWrapping="Wrap"
    VerticalAlignment="Top" FontSize="32">
        <Run Text="Some Text"/>
        <LineBreak/>
        <Run Text="More  Text"/>
        <LineBreak/>
        <Run Text="Some "/>
        <Run Text="more text"/>
        <LineBreak/>
        <Run Text="lots of text"/>
        <LineBreak/>
        <Run Text="......."/>
    </TextBlock>
    </Grid>
</Page>
```

Scalable Assets

When you take a photo with a 24-megapixel camera and view it on a 1080p display, how does it work? How does it scale down? Or when you take a photo with an old 2-megapixel mobile camera and view it on a gorgeous display like in Microsoft Surface Studio, how does the image scale up? Even when you resize an app's window, the images adjust accordingly. First, let's examine scaling and then move forward with scalable assets in a UWP app.

There are several algorithms out there for scaling, such as linear and bicubic scaling. Let's say your output display requires a space four times larger than you have in the image. What linear scaling will do is multiply each pixel by a factor of 4, as shown in Table 4-1. After scaling, some sort of sharpening is often done so that the scaled-up image does not look blurred and crappy. This is how the software zoom in camera applications works.

Table 4-1. *Example of an Original 2x2 Pixels on the Left (first two columns) and Linearly Scaled 4x4 Pixels on the Right (last four columns)*

		70	70	200	200
70	200	70	70	200	200
127	4	127	127	4	4
		127	127	4	4

■ **Note**   An image captured from optical zoom is the actual data and an image captured from software zoom is a scaled and sharpened version of the image captured.

This is one reason why hardware manufacturers keep putting in better lenses and sensors: to capture more and more megapixels with your phone camera.

Now let's come back to Universal Windows. It's for everyone, as in variable devices with variable output displays and variable processors. We cannot use a very high resolution, optically zoomed-in image because scaling it down by a large factor is a problem with low-end devices with low energy-consuming mobile processors. For instance, if you have a 4000x4000 spatial resolution color image and you are scaling it down, the hardware is essentially working with 4000x4000, which is 16 million pixels, and each pixel has RGB data so 16x3 = 48 million data values. And you can't use a low-resolution image because digitally scaling and sharpening an image looks terrible on high-end displays.

This has been addressed by UWP's scalable assets. A developer puts various spatial resolution versions of the same image and Windows picks the closest match to use (the one that require minimum scaling). The same concept applies to your own assets in your app as well as app icons and assets in tiles. How do you put different spatial resolution versions of the same image? It is done in a simple step via this syntax:

`<image filename>.<scale factor>.<file extension>`

Example:

`Tree.scale-50.png` is 50% scaled.
`Tree.scale-100.png` is 100% scaled (this is the intended image size).
`Tree.scale-200.png` is 200% scaled.
`Tree.scale-400.png` is 400% scaled.

And you can simply call the image with `<image filename>.<file extension>` (i.e. Tree.png).

With Visual Studio 2017, you can avoid making scalable assets for your app's tiles manually because an asset generator (shown in Figure 4-15) does it for you.

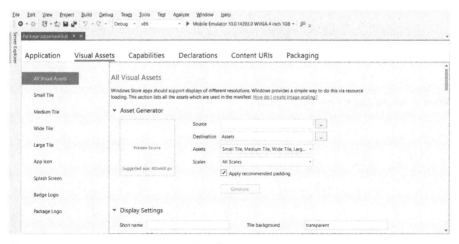

Figure 4-15. *Asset generator in Visual Studio 2017*

Custom Controls

You have come a long way and built your application UI. But now you realize that you do not like the default button appearance or you want all buttons and text boxes to adapt to the look and feel of your brand, and the whole application as a whole to feel as a part of Windows and your company/group's ecosystem. Apart from appearance, if you are using different behaviors for your controls, custom controls are the way to go. In summary, custom controls are made up of basic controls such as text boxes, buttons, and so on, and you add your own implementation such as appearances and behaviors.

To get started, you need to add a template control to your project, as shown in Figure 4-16. This will create a Generic XAML as a `ResourceDictionary` and the C# `.cs` file of your custom control. Then you define your controls in XAML and add the dependency properties of your control. You can write from scratch or create one by using `propdp` for a dependency property snippet, as shown in Figure 4-17.

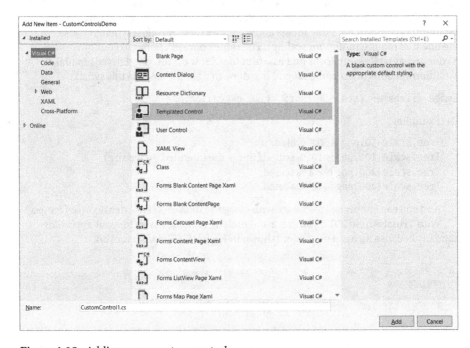

Figure 4-16. *Adding a new custom control*

```
using Windows.UI.Xaml;
using Windows.UI.Xaml.Controls;
namespace CustomControlsDemo.CustomControls
{
    public sealed class BlueButton : Control
    {
        public BlueButton()
        {
            this.DefaultStyleKey = typeof(BlueButton);
        }
        propdp
    }
        □ propdp            Define a DependencyProperty
•o ᵗₜ ᵖ ᵈ ▣ {} ≣ □      Code snippet for a property using DependencyProperty as the backing store
                         Note: Tab twice to insert the 'propdp' snippet.
}
```

Figure 4-17. *Code snippet for a dependency property*

A dependency property is a custom property you define; it extends the property of your custom control and extends the CLR properties. After defining your dependency property, you need to bind it with your XAML element using `TemplateBinding`. Data binding is covered in this chapter in a later section. For this example, you will create buttons that look like one in old Windows 95/98 or the Windows Classic look. The output is shown in Figure 4-18.

Custom Control XAML

```xml
<ResourceDictionary
    xmlns="http://schemas.microsoft.com/winfx/2006/xaml/presentation"
    xmlns:x="http://schemas.microsoft.com/winfx/2006/xaml"
    xmlns:local="using:CustomControlsDemo"
    xmlns:local2="using:CustomControlsDemo.CustomControls">
    <Style TargetType="local2:BlueButton" >
        <Setter Property="Template">
            <Setter.Value>
                <ControlTemplate TargetType="local2:BlueButton">
                    <Button Foreground="Blue" Content="{TemplateBinding
                    BlueButtonText}" HorizontalAlignment="Center"
                    BorderBrush="Blue" BorderThickness="0, 0, 1, 1"/>
                </ControlTemplate>
            </Setter.Value>
        </Setter>
    </Style>
</ResourceDictionary>
```

101

Custom Control C#

```csharp
using Windows.UI.Xaml;
using Windows.UI.Xaml.Controls;
namespace CustomControlsDemo.CustomControls
{
    public sealed class BlueButton : Control
    {
        public BlueButton()
        {
            this.DefaultStyleKey = typeof(BlueButton);
        }
        public string BlueButtonText
        {
            get { return (string)GetValue(BlueButtonTextProperty); }
            set { SetValue(BlueButtonTextProperty, value); }
        }
        public static readonly DependencyProperty BlueButtonTextProperty =
            DependencyProperty.Register("BlueButtonText", typeof(string),
            typeof(BlueButton), new PropertyMetadata(""));
    }
}
```

App XAML

```xml
<Page
    x:Class="CustomControlsDemo.MainPage"
    xmlns="http://schemas.microsoft.com/winfx/2006/xaml/presentation"
    xmlns:x="http://schemas.microsoft.com/winfx/2006/xaml"
    xmlns:local="using:CustomControlsDemo"
    xmlns:d="http://schemas.microsoft.com/expression/blend/2008"
    xmlns:mc="http://schemas.openxmlformats.org/markup-compatibility/2006"
    xmlns:customcontrols="using:CustomControlsDemo.CustomControls"
    mc:Ignorable="d">
    <Grid Background="{ThemeResource ApplicationPageBackgroundThemeBrush}">
        <Grid.RowDefinitions>
            <RowDefinition/>
            <RowDefinition Height="100"/>
        </Grid.RowDefinitions>
        <customcontrols:BlueButton Grid.Row="1" BlueButtonText="My Button"
        Grid.RowSpan="2" HorizontalAlignment="Right" Margin="0,0,130,0"/>
        <customcontrols:BlueButton Grid.Row="1" BlueButtonText="My Button 2"
        Grid.RowSpan="2" HorizontalAlignment="Right" Margin="0,0,10,0"/>
        <TextBlock HorizontalAlignment="Center" Margin="0,10,0,0"
        TextWrapping="Wrap" Text="Custom Controls Demo"
        VerticalAlignment="Top"/>
    </Grid>
</Page>
```

Figure 4-18. Output of custom control application

Code Behind

Code behind is whatever you do in your back-end C# code: your business logic implementation, variables, structures, enumeration, etc. Universal Windows Platform applications implement the **MVVM (model-view-ViewModel)** architectural pattern. The front-end XAML is the view, the code behind is the model or your business model, and the thing connecting the model and view is the ViewModel, such as with events. Let's explore this concept by using a professional camera. The view would then be what you see on the digital display or in older camera models: the dial to change modes like aperture priority. The model is the built-in software to control the camera shutter. And the ViewModel is the thing connecting these two and what makes the model perform based on your shooting preference.

You saw a lot of C# code behind in the previous sections. In this section, I will cover a bit more. In this section, you are not going to touch the front end but instead you will work with the code behind only in order to understand some of the concepts. You are going to implement an enum and struct. You can create an enumeration list using enum.

It is a list of distinct elements in your application. If you were building a paint application, your enum list would contain the list of different brush textures like pencil, pen, chalk, water ink, etc. Let's look at the code to understand.

C#

```
using System.Collections.Generic;
using System.Diagnostics;
using Windows.UI.Xaml.Controls;
namespace CodeBehindDemo
{
    public sealed partial class MainPage : Page
    {
        public MainPage()
        {
            this.InitializeComponent();
            people person1 = new people("Joey", month.February);
            people person2 = new people("Amanda", month.June);
            Debug.WriteLine(person1.name);
            Debug.WriteLine(person2.name);
        }
    }
    public enum month
    {
        January,
        February,
        March,
        April,
        May,
        June,
        July,
        August,
        Septeber,
        October,
        November,
        December
    }
    public struct people
    {
        public string name;
        public month birthMonth;
        public people(string n, month bm)
        {
            name = n;
            birthMonth = bm;
        }
    }
}
```

You have created an enumeration list for a month because they are definite and you wish to narrow it down. Giving the month input as input can enable made-up month inputs like Wordenary. And you have created a structure to store a person's name and birth month, the output of which is shown in Figure 4-19.

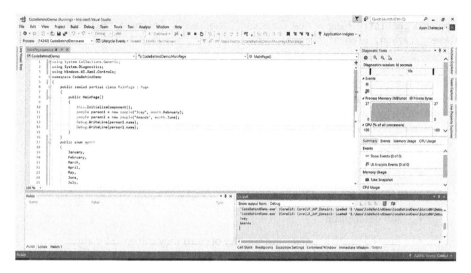

Figure 4-19. *Output of the code behind application demo*

If that example did not clear up the concept, let's take a look at high school chemistry. We all know the basic elements are hydrogen, helium, lithium, and oxygen, and that they form compounds like carbon monoxide (CO), carbon dioxide (CO_2), and so on. An enum list would consist of what is possible, the basic elements in the periodic table:

```
enum elements
{
        hydrogen, helium, lithium, oxygen, carbon, magnesium, iron
}
```

And compounds would form a structure like

```
struct compound
{
        string commonName;
        elements[] composition;
        int[] abundancy;
        compound(string name, elements[] com, int[] mixures)
        {
                commonName = name;
                composition = com;
                abundancy = mixtures;
        }
}
```

And all of the existing and even newly invented chemical compounds can then be stored in an orderly fashion. Composition and abundancies are an array because there can be more than one element making up a chemical compound. I am not a chemist, but for explanation purposes, let's create a chemical compound with composition He_2CO_5. The syntax is

```
compound chemistryThing = new compound("someName", [element.helium,
element.carbon, element,oxygen], [2, 1, 5]);
```

An *interface*, on the hand, does not do anything. It is more of a declaration of a standard to follow. To explain this more, let's take a look at an employment contract that companies make any employee sign, be it a full-time employment agreement or a work-for-hire agreement. Before moving to a formal statement, let's explore the possible contents.

Interface Employee

- Name of company

- Name of employee

- Legal addresses of both parties

- Job description

- Legal domain like state and country of court they will go to for any conflict

- Benefits like healthcare

Interface FullTime

- Additional benefits of a full-time employee

- Annual salary

- Holidays and leave days

- Notice period to quit

Interface WorkForHire

- Deadline or termination of contract

- Periodic milestones

- Payment for the job

Now if you implement a class to include interfaces, the class is obliged by a binding contract to implement everything declared within the interface. More than one interface can be implemented within a class as well. For instance, a full-time employee (say Tom) would implement

```
class Tom : Employee, FullTime
```

A temporary employee named Tim would implement

```
class Tim : Employee, WorkForHire
```

As a common custom among developers, an interface is named starting with I to quickly identify that it is an interface. Some of them are IList, ICollection, IEnumerable, IEnumarator, etc. Let's try an implementation, the output of which is shown in Figure 4-20.

Interface

```
using Windows.UI.Xaml.Media;
namespace InterfaceDemo.CustomStuff
{
    interface IMaterial
    {
        double GetMaterialReflectance(materials material, double wavelength);
        materialType GetMaterialType(materials material);
        SolidColorBrush GetMaterialColor(materials material);
    }
}
```

C# (Class using the interface)

```
using Windows.UI;
using Windows.UI.Xaml.Media;
namespace InterfaceDemo.CustomStuff
{
    public enum materials
    {
        Iron,
        Ceramic,
        Grass,
        Tree,
        Ice,
        Water,
        Mud,
        Aluminium
    }
    public enum materialType
    {
        solid,
        liquid,
        gas
    }
    class Definitions : IMaterial
    {
        public SolidColorBrush GetMaterialColor(materials material)
        {
            return new SolidColorBrush(Color.FromArgb(255, 165, 210, 100));
            //dummy color used
        }
```

```csharp
        public double GetMaterialReflectance(materials material, double wavelength)
        {
            return 0.9; //dummy reflectance used
        }

        public materialType GetMaterialType(materials material)
        {
            switch (material)
            {
                case materials.Aluminium: //taking advantage of fall down property
                case materials.Ceramic:
                case materials.Grass:
                case materials.Ice:
                case materials.Iron:
                case materials.Tree: return materialType.solid;
                case materials.Water: return materialType.liquid;
            }
            return materialType.gas;
        }
    }
}
```

C# (Main Page)

```csharp
using Windows.UI.Xaml.Controls;
using InterfaceDemo.CustomStuff;
using System.Diagnostics;
namespace InterfaceDemo
{
    public sealed partial class MainPage : Page
    {
        public MainPage()
        {
            this.InitializeComponent();
            Definitions mat1 = new Definitions();
            Debug.WriteLine(mat1.GetMaterialType(materials.Ice).ToString());
            Debug.WriteLine(mat1.GetMaterialType(materials.Water).ToString());
        }
    }
}
```

Figure 4-20. Output of the Interface application displayed in debug window

Data Binding

With data binding, as the name says, you are trying to bind or relate one element's data to another. The binding can be with a single object like turning the visibility on and off of a grid to the value of a toggle or to a collection of objects like the values of a drop-down menu. Every binding has a binding source and binding target, and can be one-time, one-way, or two-way binding.

One-time binding occurs only once and doesn't update during runtime. One-way binding only updates the destination with changes in the source. Two-way binding makes changes in both directions. You can do this both in XAML and code behind. If you are doing this in XAML, you can use either {Binding} or {x:Bind}, or by making a class observable in code behind using the INotifyPropertyChanged interface and implementing the property PropertyChanged. If you recall the discussion on interfaces, this will be simple for you. Let's create a data binding between a grid and a toggle button using Blend, as shown in Figures 4-21 and 4-22.

■ **Tip** Binding a lot of UIElements may slow down your application and make it unresponsive because with every data binding definition the system allocates some resources to wait and listen for changes.

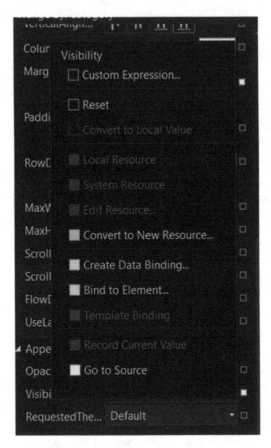

Figure 4-21. Data binding options in Blend when you click the square shape at the side of each property

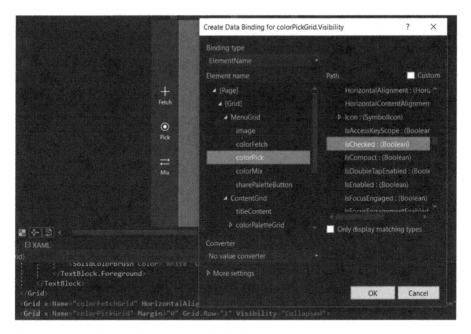

Figure 4-22. *Grid visibility binding with the Boolean value of Checked property of a toggle button*

Animations and Transitions

Transitions occur to reveal the elements in a page, whereas *animations* occur while the page is active. Animations can be triggered automatically by the main function or manually when triggered by a user's action. The animations that are most often used in UWP applications are storyboard animations. Storyboards can either be created from code behind or via a simpler approach, through Blend. Let's walk through the steps to create a simple storyboard animation in Blend and also a transition in XAML.

However, let's first discuss animations. Living in the digital age we have all seen animations occur in films, games, apps, vlogs, news, while watching sports on television, and pretty much everywhere. But how are they made? Creating storyboard animations for UWP applications is not much different from how professionals animate using applications like Adobe Animate. Let's say there's a circular object with a radius of 5 centimeters and in 10 seconds you want to make it 10 centimeters. To make this into an animation, you place the circular object on the scene and define the following:

> Time 0s: (called start frame in this scenario)
>
> Radius of circular object = 5 cm
>
> Time 10s: (called end frame in this scenario)
>
> Radius of curricular object = 10 cm

That's it! The animation software fills all of the intermediate paths. So, for 1 second the radius would have increased linearly to $5 + (10 - 5)/10 = 5.5$ cm. Now let's dive into storyboard animations using Blend for Visual Studio. For this example, you will place three ellipses and a text block in the scene in Blend, as shown in Figure 4-23.

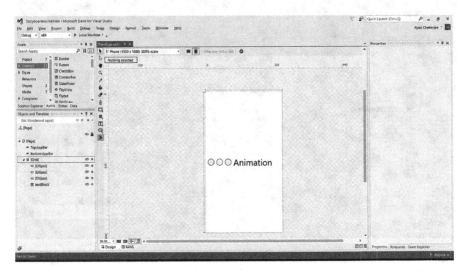

Figure 4-23. *Assets placed on the workspace prior to creating an animation*

To create a new storyboard, click the + button shown in Figure 4-24. This will open up a new pop-up window where you need to enter the name of your storyboard, as shown in Figure 4-25.

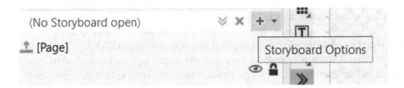

Figure 4-24. *Use the + button to create a new storyboard*

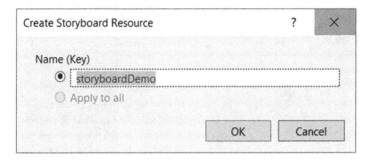

Figure 4-25. *Naming the storyboard*

Once you have created your storyboard, a timeline appears in Blend, as shown in Figure 4-26. If you have worked with any 2D or 3D animation software like Adobe Animate or Autodesk Maya, this part should be familiar to you. To create an animation, you change the values of the start frame, end frame, and the intermediate frames where significant changes occur; the rest are filled in automatically during runtime.

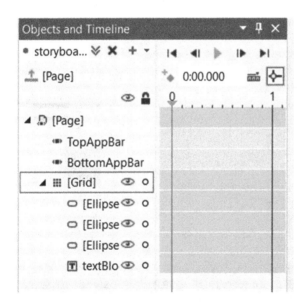

Figure 4-26. *Storyboard animation timeline*

With the storyboard timeline created, you should change the properties of the elements to match Figures 4-27, 4-28, and 4-29. Thereafter, you will change the repeat behavior of the storyboard animation (Figure 4-30) by clicking the storyboard and changing properties.

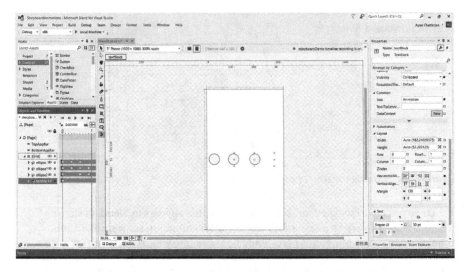

Figure 4-27. *Changing the property of an asset (hiding the text) in a timeline to create an animation*

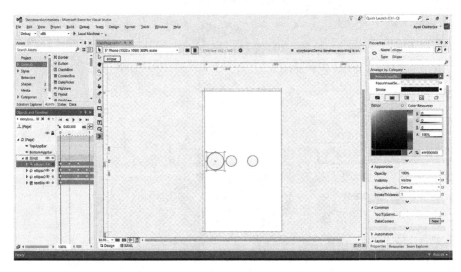

Figure 4-28. *Changing the property of an asset (radius of the first circle) in the timeline to create an animation*

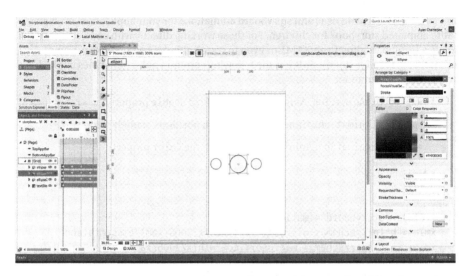

Figure 4-29. *Changing the property of an asset (radius of the second circle) in the timeline to create an animation*

Figure 4-30. *Repeat behavior of your animation*

115

You can now create beautiful storyboard animations for your application, even an entire animated storybook for children. For those working directly with code, you may create a storyboard directly in XAML or even in code behind. The Windows runtime animation system for storyboards has the following common animation types applied over a specified duration:

- DoubleAnimation: Animating values with a double property

- PointAnimation: Animating values with positions, namely x and y

- ColorAnimation: Animating values with the Color property

XAML

```
<Page
    x:Class="StoryboardAnimations.MainPage"
    xmlns="http://schemas.microsoft.com/winfx/2006/xaml/presentation"
    xmlns:x="http://schemas.microsoft.com/winfx/2006/xaml"
    xmlns:local="using:StoryboardAnimations"
    xmlns:d="http://schemas.microsoft.com/expression/blend/2008"
    xmlns:mc="http://schemas.openxmlformats.org/markup-compatibility/2006"
    mc:Ignorable="d">
    <Page.Resources>
        <Storyboard x:Name="storyboardDemo" RepeatBehavior="Forever">
            <ObjectAnimationUsingKeyFrames Storyboard.TargetProperty=
            "(UIElement.Visibility)" Storyboard.TargetName="textBlock">
                <DiscreteObjectKeyFrame KeyTime="0">
                    <DiscreteObjectKeyFrame.Value>
                        <Visibility>Collapsed</Visibility>
                    </DiscreteObjectKeyFrame.Value>
                </DiscreteObjectKeyFrame>
                <DiscreteObjectKeyFrame KeyTime="0:0:1.2">
                    <DiscreteObjectKeyFrame.Value>
                        <Visibility>Visible</Visibility>
                    </DiscreteObjectKeyFrame.Value>
                </DiscreteObjectKeyFrame>
                <DiscreteObjectKeyFrame KeyTime="0:0:2">
                    <DiscreteObjectKeyFrame.Value>
                        <Visibility>Collapsed</Visibility>
                    </DiscreteObjectKeyFrame.Value>
                </DiscreteObjectKeyFrame>
            </ObjectAnimationUsingKeyFrames>
            <DoubleAnimationUsingKeyFrames EnableDependentAnimation="True"
            Storyboard.TargetProperty="(FrameworkElement.Width)" Storyboard.
            TargetName="ellipse">
                <EasingDoubleKeyFrame KeyTime="0" Value="50"/>
                <EasingDoubleKeyFrame KeyTime="0:0:0.3" Value="80"/>
                <EasingDoubleKeyFrame KeyTime="0:0:0.6" Value="50"/>
                <EasingDoubleKeyFrame KeyTime="0:0:1.2" Value="30"/>
```

```xml
</DoubleAnimationUsingKeyFrames>
<DoubleAnimationUsingKeyFrames EnableDependentAnimation="True"
Storyboard.TargetProperty="(FrameworkElement.Width)" Storyboard.
TargetName="ellipse1">
    <EasingDoubleKeyFrame KeyTime="0" Value="50"/>
    <EasingDoubleKeyFrame KeyTime="0:0:0.3" Value="50"/>
    <EasingDoubleKeyFrame KeyTime="0:0:0.6" Value="80"/>
    <EasingDoubleKeyFrame KeyTime="0:0:0.9" Value="50"/>
    <EasingDoubleKeyFrame KeyTime="0:0:1.2" Value="30"/>
</DoubleAnimationUsingKeyFrames>
<DoubleAnimationUsingKeyFrames EnableDependentAnimation="True"
Storyboard.TargetProperty="(FrameworkElement.Width)" Storyboard.
TargetName="ellipse2">
    <EasingDoubleKeyFrame KeyTime="0" Value="50"/>
    <EasingDoubleKeyFrame KeyTime="0:0:0.6" Value="50"/>
    <EasingDoubleKeyFrame KeyTime="0:0:0.9" Value="80"/>
    <EasingDoubleKeyFrame KeyTime="0:0:1.2" Value="30"/>
</DoubleAnimationUsingKeyFrames>
<DoubleAnimationUsingKeyFrames EnableDependentAnimation="True"
Storyboard.TargetProperty="(FrameworkElement.Height)"
Storyboard.TargetName="ellipse">
    <EasingDoubleKeyFrame KeyTime="0" Value="50"/>
    <EasingDoubleKeyFrame KeyTime="0:0:0.3" Value="80"/>
    <EasingDoubleKeyFrame KeyTime="0:0:0.6" Value="50"/>
    <EasingDoubleKeyFrame KeyTime="0:0:1.2" Value="30"/>
</DoubleAnimationUsingKeyFrames>
<DoubleAnimationUsingKeyFrames EnableDependentAnimation="True"
Storyboard.TargetProperty="(FrameworkElement.Height)"
Storyboard.TargetName="ellipse1">
    <EasingDoubleKeyFrame KeyTime="0" Value="50"/>
    <EasingDoubleKeyFrame KeyTime="0:0:0.3" Value="50"/>
    <EasingDoubleKeyFrame KeyTime="0:0:0.6" Value="80"/>
    <EasingDoubleKeyFrame KeyTime="0:0:0.9" Value="50"/>
    <EasingDoubleKeyFrame KeyTime="0:0:1.2" Value="30"/>
</DoubleAnimationUsingKeyFrames>
<DoubleAnimationUsingKeyFrames EnableDependentAnimation="True"
Storyboard.TargetProperty="(FrameworkElement.Height)"
Storyboard.TargetName="ellipse2">
    <EasingDoubleKeyFrame KeyTime="0" Value="50"/>
    <EasingDoubleKeyFrame KeyTime="0:0:0.6" Value="50"/>
    <EasingDoubleKeyFrame KeyTime="0:0:0.9" Value="80"/>
    <EasingDoubleKeyFrame KeyTime="0:0:1.2" Value="30"/>
</DoubleAnimationUsingKeyFrames>
<ObjectAnimationUsingKeyFrames Storyboard.TargetProperty=
"(FrameworkElement.Margin)" Storyboard.TargetName="ellipse1">
    <DiscreteObjectKeyFrame KeyTime="0">
        <DiscreteObjectKeyFrame.Value>
            <Thickness>100,0,0,0</Thickness>
```

```
                    </DiscreteObjectKeyFrame.Value>
                </DiscreteObjectKeyFrame>
                <DiscreteObjectKeyFrame KeyTime="0:0:0.9">
                    <DiscreteObjectKeyFrame.Value>
                        <Thickness>50,0,0,0</Thickness>
                    </DiscreteObjectKeyFrame.Value>
                </DiscreteObjectKeyFrame>
                <DiscreteObjectKeyFrame KeyTime="0:0:1.2">
                    <DiscreteObjectKeyFrame.Value>
                        <Thickness>51,0,0,0</Thickness>
                    </DiscreteObjectKeyFrame.Value>
                </DiscreteObjectKeyFrame>
            </ObjectAnimationUsingKeyFrames>
            <ObjectAnimationUsingKeyFrames Storyboard.TargetProperty=
            "(FrameworkElement.Margin)" Storyboard.TargetName="ellipse2">
                <DiscreteObjectKeyFrame KeyTime="0">
                    <DiscreteObjectKeyFrame.Value>
                        <Thickness>200,0,0,0</Thickness>
                    </DiscreteObjectKeyFrame.Value>
                </DiscreteObjectKeyFrame>
                <DiscreteObjectKeyFrame KeyTime="0:0:0.9">
                    <DiscreteObjectKeyFrame.Value>
                        <Thickness>90,0,0,0</Thickness>
                    </DiscreteObjectKeyFrame.Value>
                </DiscreteObjectKeyFrame>
                <DiscreteObjectKeyFrame KeyTime="0:0:1.2">
                    <DiscreteObjectKeyFrame.Value>
                        <Thickness>91,0,0,0</Thickness>
                    </DiscreteObjectKeyFrame.Value>
                </DiscreteObjectKeyFrame>
            </ObjectAnimationUsingKeyFrames>
            <DoubleAnimationUsingKeyFrames EnableDependentAnimation="True"
            Storyboard.TargetProperty="(FrameworkElement.FocusVisualPrimaryBrush).
            (Brush.Opacity)" Storyboard.TargetName="textBlock">
                <EasingDoubleKeyFrame KeyTime="0" Value="1"/>
                <EasingDoubleKeyFrame KeyTime="0:0:1.2" Value="1"/>
            </DoubleAnimationUsingKeyFrames>
        </Storyboard>
    </Page.Resources>

    <Grid Background="{ThemeResource ApplicationPageBackgroundThemeBrush}">
        <Ellipse x:Name="ellipse" Fill="#FFF4F4F5" HorizontalAlignment=
        "Left" Margin="10,0,0,0" Stroke="Black" Width="30" Height="30"
        VerticalAlignment="Center"/>
        <Ellipse x:Name="ellipse1" Fill="#FFF4F4F5"
        HorizontalAlignment="Left" Margin="50,0,0,0" Stroke="Black"
        Width="30" Height="30" VerticalAlignment="Center"/>
```

```
<Ellipse x:Name="ellipse2" Fill="#FFF4F4F5"
HorizontalAlignment="Left" Height="30" Margin="90,0,0,0"
Stroke="Black" VerticalAlignment="Center" Width="30"/>
<TextBlock x:Name="textBlock" Margin="130,0,0,0" TextWrapping=
"Wrap" Text="Animation" d:LayoutOverrides="Width, Height"
HorizontalAlignment="Left" VerticalAlignment="Center" FontSize="40"/>

    </Grid>
</Page>
```

C#

```
using Windows.UI.Xaml.Controls;
using Windows.UI.Xaml.Navigation;

namespace StoryboardAnimations
{
    public sealed partial class MainPage : Page
    {
        public MainPage()
        {
            this.InitializeComponent();
            storyboardDemo.Begin(); //to start the storyboard animation
        }
        protected override void OnNavigatingFrom(NavigatingCancelEventArgs e)
        {
            storyboardDemo.Stop(); //to stop the animation
        }
    }
}
```

Files in the File System

Why are there so many different file extensions? For instance, there are jpeg, png, gif, and tiff extensions for images; obj, 3ds, and sldprt for 3D files; mpg, avi, mp4, and mkv for video; and the list goes on and on. Some are open and some are proprietary. But why are there so many different options for a single thing? Wouldn't one format for an image, one for video, and one for a 3D file make everyone's life easier? Individual file structure, encoding, compression, and encryption algorithms are some of the elements that play a role in the uniqueness of a file.

Let's take one element as an example: memory allocation. Suppose in your program that you use 8-bit integers to store some data, while someone else (say Tim) uses the double data type for more accuracy. While your justification may be to make your app run faster and save memory, Tim wants accuracy and is not bothered about saving memory. Table 4-2 shows the differences on just 16 units of data.

Table 4-2. *Comparison of Outputs with Different Data Types*

Data Type	8-bit integer	double	String
Output file	Binary	Binary	Text
File size	16 bytes	128 bytes	41 bytes (56 bytes with spaces added between the numbers)
Data units	16	16	16
How it looks in Notepad application	ÝE|7˜aÁ)ŠsÏ³n¥	ⅱ ⅱ ⅰ ⅱ ⅰ ⅰ ⅱ ⅱ ⅱ ⅱ ⅱ ⅱ ⅰ ⅱ ⅰ	221 28 41 179 69 152 138 110 124 97 83 165 55 193 207 14

Because Notepad is designed to read text, others look like noise. Similarly, to read the right data from a file, you need to know the structure and other details. Note how changing just a data type from integer to double or string changes the file size drastically.

Major industrial software applications store data in the same way. If you recall the concepts like structures and arrays covered earlier, a personalized music/video player application can store some data to make the app pick up where the user left off with each song/playlist. The way you do it is completely your decision, but Figure 4-31 shows a way to store an audio file and playlist information. To implement Figure 4-31 and store thousands of playlists as a storage file, you can make a tabular structure or even simply store them as a text file and put in your own file extension, so when you search for it you know which file extension to look for. The following is an example (let's call it myPopSongs.playlist):

```
Name = "My Pop Songs"
Songs = {"D:/Music/Pop1.mp3", "D:/Music/pop2.mp3", "D:/Music/pop3.mp3"}
LastPlayed = {2, 0:53}
```

Figure 4-31 shows how to design your application to be more efficient and store simple or even complex files.

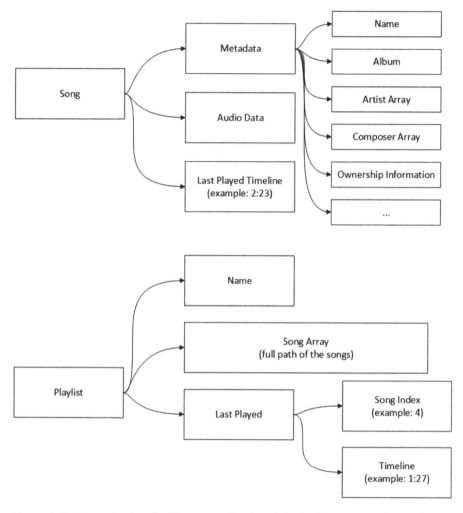

Figure 4-31. *Example of audio file structure (top) and playlist file structure (bottom)*

Globalization and Localization

You have taken the time to read this book and to build a UWP app. This shows that you believe in your product(s). Whatever you are building is for the people to experience. If you limit your application to one language, you are limiting your app to a certain region. For instance, if you have written all the text boxes and text blocks and button text in English, your audience is limited to the United States, the United Kingdom, Canada, and some percentage of English literates in other non-English speaking countries.

If your application is not limited to a specific community speaking a single language, you might want to consider using globalization and localization in your UWP application to reach the rest of the world. The terms *globalization* and *localization* represents language and cultural changes in languages. What does *cultural change* mean? A couple of examples are shown below to demonstrate cultural differences within the English language.

- Weight: Kilogram, pound, stone

- Currency: Dollar, pound

- Distance: Kilometer, mile

- Within school grading system: GPA, percentage, class

- Spellings: Centre, center

- Date: Day/month/year or month/day/year

There exists cultural change from region to region. Some foreign languages are read/written from right to left. Some of them have calendars that do not follow January to December.

To globalize your application, first define x:Uid of your UIElements, similar to how you do it with x:Name. Then create a folder named Strings, and then folders for every language like en-US for American English, en-GB for British English, fr-FR for French (France), and so on, as shown in Figure 4-32. Then add a Resources file for each. In the resources file, you put in the name-value pair data, as shown in Figure 4-33. For this example, you will be using this book's marketing material (title and description) because it contains a lot of text. And to differentiate from en-US and en-GB, simply add (US) and (GB) in the title to see which language Windows is running. The output is shown in Figure 4-34.

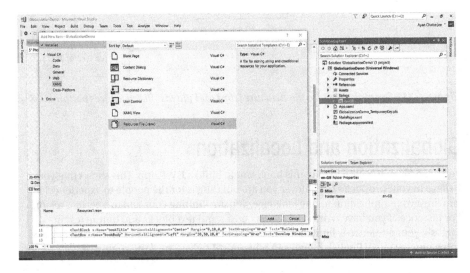

Figure 4-32. *Creating a resource file*

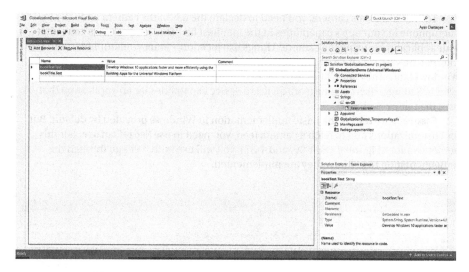

Figure 4-33. Adding name-value pairs to resources

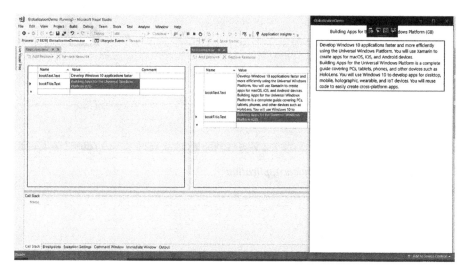

Figure 4-34. Output of the globalized application for two languages

Camera and Media Capture Devices

I have talked a lot about images and what to do with them once the data is captured, but I haven't talked about how to capture the data. This section explores how you can capture the data from a camera attached to your Windows device.

To enable a user's camera, you need to declare the use of the camera and microphone in your app's capabilities in the manifest file. This lets the users know that your application is using the camera. Things like location, camera, microphone, and the Internet are very sensitive subjects in terms of user privacy. When downloading from Windows Store, the capabilities used by an application are displayed in the Store and even in Settings. Users can turn on/off these device capabilities for an application that uses them from Settings.

CameraCaptureUI is the basic implementation in Windows provided by default. But for customizations and to fetch a camera feed, you need to use MediaCapture. For this demonstration (Figures 4-35, 4-36, and 4-37), you will use both. Let's go through the implementation to see how they are implemented.

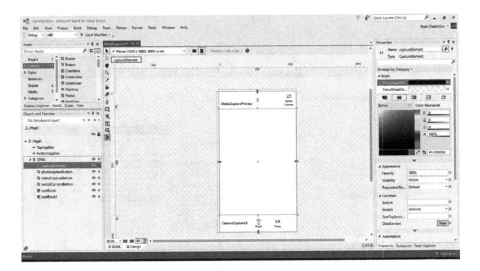

Figure 4-35. UI of Camera Preview application

Figure 4-36. *MediaCapture implementation*

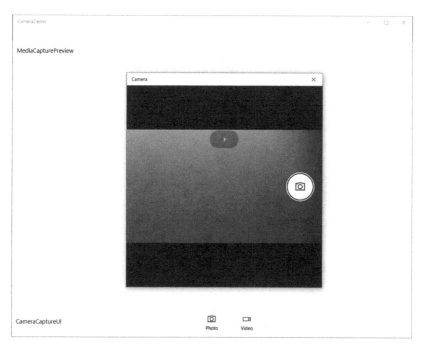

Figure 4-37. *CameraCaptureUI implementation*

XAML

```xml
<Page
    x:Class="CameraDemo.MainPage"
    xmlns="http://schemas.microsoft.com/winfx/2006/xaml/presentation"
    xmlns:x="http://schemas.microsoft.com/winfx/2006/xaml"
    xmlns:local="using:CameraDemo"
    xmlns:d="http://schemas.microsoft.com/expression/blend/2008"
    xmlns:mc="http://schemas.openxmlformats.org/markup-compatibility/2006"
    mc:Ignorable="d">

    <Grid Background="{ThemeResource ApplicationPageBackgroundThemeBrush}">
        <CaptureElement x:Name="captureElement" Margin="0,80"/>
        <AppBarButton x:Name="photocaptureButton" Click="photocaptureButton_
        Click" Icon="Camera" Label="Photo" d:LayoutOverrides="Width"
        VerticalAlignment="Bottom" HorizontalAlignment="Center"
        Margin="0,0,0,10"/>
        <AppBarButton x:Name="videoCaptureButton" Click="videoCaptureButton_
        Click" Icon="Video" Label="Video" d:LayoutOverrides="Width"
        Margin="180,0,0,10" VerticalAlignment="Bottom"
        HorizontalAlignment="Center"/>
        <AppBarButton x:Name="switchCameraButton" Click="switchCameraButton_
        Click" Icon="Switch" Label="Switch Camera" d:LayoutOverrides="Width"
        HorizontalAlignment="Right" Visibility="Collapsed"/>
        <TextBlock x:Name="textBlock" HorizontalAlignment="Left"
        Margin="10,46,0,0" TextWrapping="Wrap" Text="MediaCapturePreview"
        VerticalAlignment="Top"/>
        <TextBlock x:Name="textBlock1" HorizontalAlignment="Left"
        Margin="10,0,0,30" TextWrapping="Wrap" Text="CameraCaptureUI"
        VerticalAlignment="Bottom"/>
    </Grid>
</Page>
```

C#

```csharp
using System;
using Windows.Devices.Enumeration;
using Windows.Media.Capture;
using Windows.Storage;
using Windows.UI.Xaml.Controls;
namespace CameraDemo
{
    public sealed partial class MainPage : Page
    {
        int elem = -1;
        DeviceInformationCollection devices;
        MediaCapture mc = new MediaCapture();
        public MainPage()
```

```
{
    this.InitializeComponent();
    initializeCamera();
}

private async void initializeCamera()
{
    devices = await DeviceInformation.FindAllAsync(DeviceClass.
    VideoCapture);
    if(devices.Count > 1)
    {
        switchCameraButton.Visibility = Windows.UI.Xaml.Visibility.Visible;
    }
    if(devices.Count > 0)
    {
        elem = 0;
        MediaCaptureInitializationSettings mcSettings =
        new MediaCaptureInitializationSettings { VideoDeviceId =
        devices[elem].Id, StreamingCaptureMode =
        StreamingCaptureMode.Video};
        await mc.InitializeAsync(mcSettings);
        captureElement.Source = mc;
        await mc.StartPreviewAsync();
    }
}
private async void photocaptureButton_Click(object sender,
Windows.UI.Xaml.RoutedEventArgs e)
{
    await mc.StopPreviewAsync();
    CameraCaptureUI camera = new CameraCaptureUI();
    camera.PhotoSettings.Format = CameraCaptureUIPhotoFormat.Jpeg;
    StorageFile photo = await camera.CaptureFileAsync(CameraCapture
    UIMode.Photo);
    if(photo != null)
        await photo.MoveAsync(KnownFolders.PicturesLibrary,
        "new_photo.jpeg", NameCollisionOption.GenerateUniqueName);
    await mc.StartPreviewAsync();
}
private async void videoCaptureButton_Click(object sender,
Windows.UI.Xaml.RoutedEventArgs e)
{
    await mc.StopPreviewAsync();
    CameraCaptureUI camera = new CameraCaptureUI();
    camera.VideoSettings.Format = CameraCaptureUIVideoFormat.Mp4;
    StorageFile video = await camera.CaptureFileAsync(CameraCapture
    UIMode.Video);
    if (video != null)
```

```
            await video.MoveAsync(KnownFolders.VideosLibrary,
                "new_video.mp4", NameCollisionOption.GenerateUniqueName);
        await mc.StartPreviewAsync();
    }

    private async void switchCameraButton_Click(object sender,
    Windows.UI.Xaml.RoutedEventArgs e)
    {
        await mc.StopPreviewAsync();
        mc.Dispose();
        MediaCapture mcNew = new MediaCapture();
        elem = elem < devices.Count - 1 ? elem + 1 : 0;
        MediaCaptureInitializationSettings mcSettings = new
        MediaCaptureInitializationSettings { VideoDeviceId = devices[elem].
        Id, StreamingCaptureMode = StreamingCaptureMode.Video };
        await mcNew.InitializeAsync(mcSettings);
        captureElement.Source = mcNew;
        await mcNew.StartPreviewAsync();
        mc = mcNew;
    }
  }
}
```

Securing App Data

Let's discuss cryptography before diving into this section. During early and sometimes even in late teen ages, people tend to develop some kind of code among their friends. For instance, when adults walk in on a private conversation, they may slip in the word "pal" into a sentence, which is code for "parents are listening/" This is a something all of these teens understand, so everyone instantly censors the conversation without making the adult aware of it. Other code types include hand gestures or newly invented words/ phrases. Let's look at the same concept in a diagram (Figure 4-38).

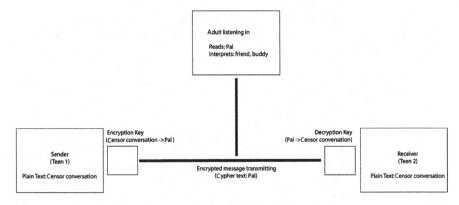

Figure 4-38. *Explanation for encryption and decryption process*

This example was to illustrate the point. For data, encryption and decryption are done through algorithms, meaning they are mathematical equations. Let's discuss a very simple one at first called Caesar Cipher; it moves up or down a character by a certain number of steps. For example, let's move up by two steps (a -> c, b -> d, etc.):

```
Input Text = How was your day
Encrypted Text = Jqy ycu aqwt fca
```

The key used during encryption and decryption may be the same (called symmetric keys) or they may be different (asymmetric keys). Table 4-3 shows the methods used in UWP and their description.

Table 4-3. *Methods for Encryption and Decryption*

Method	Description
ProtectAsync(Windows.Storage.Streams.IBuffer)	Protects static data
UnprotectAsync(Windows.Storage.Streams.IBuffer)	Unprotects static data
ProtectStreamAsync(Windows.Storage.Streams.IInputStream, Windows.Storage.Streams.IOutputStream)	Protects stream data
UnprotectStreamAsync(Windows.Storage.Streams.IInputStream, Windows.Storage.Streams.IOutputStream)	Unprotects stream data

DataProtectionProvider represents the cryptographic provider for encryption. It shows who has and can encrypt and decrypt the data. For your example, you will be using local user. Others are local machine, and web authentication for your application to be available in Windows Store. Enterprise users working on company accounts will use SID or SDDL providers and will require enterprise authentication capability. Let's implement an application that encrypts/decrypts static data (text) and see how it is done. The output is shown in Figure 4-39.

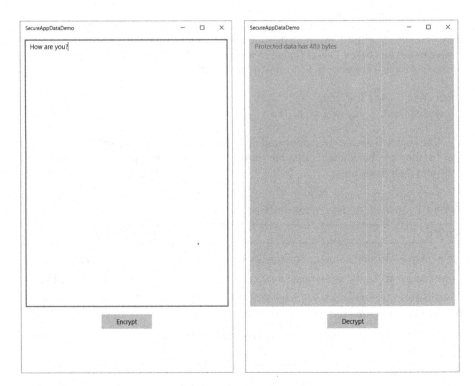

Figure 4-39. *Text before and after encryption*

XAML

```
<Page
    x:Class="SecureAppDataDemo.MainPage"
    xmlns="http://schemas.microsoft.com/winfx/2006/xaml/presentation"
    xmlns:x="http://schemas.microsoft.com/winfx/2006/xaml"
    xmlns:local="using:SecureAppDataDemo"
    xmlns:d="http://schemas.microsoft.com/expression/blend/2008"
    xmlns:mc="http://schemas.openxmlformats.org/markup-compatibility/2006"
    mc:Ignorable="d">

    <Grid Background="{ThemeResource ApplicationPageBackgroundThemeBrush}">
        <TextBox x:Name="plainTextBox" TextChanged="plainTextBox_TextChanged"
        Margin="10,10,10,150" TextWrapping="Wrap" Text="" AcceptsReturn="True"
        PlaceholderText="type your plain text here"/>
        <Button x:Name="secureButton" Click="secureButton_Click" IsEnabled=
        "False" Content="Encrypt" Margin="0,0,0,100" VerticalAlignment=
        "Bottom" HorizontalAlignment="Center" Width="120"/>
    </Grid>
</Page>
```

C#

```
using System;
using Windows.Storage.Streams;
using Windows.UI.Xaml.Controls;
using Windows.Security.Cryptography;
using Windows.Security.Cryptography.DataProtection;

namespace SecureAppDataDemo
{
    public sealed partial class MainPage : Page
    {
        string text;
        bool encrypt = true;
        IBuffer protectedData;
        public MainPage()
        {
            this.InitializeComponent();
        }
        private void plainTextBox_TextChanged(object sender,
        TextChangedEventArgs e)
        {
            text = plainTextBox.Text;
            secureButton.IsEnabled = (text != null || text != "") ? true : false;
        }
        private async void secureButton_Click(object sender, Windows.
        UI.Xaml.RoutedEventArgs e)
        {
            if (encrypt)
            {
                BinaryStringEncoding encoding = BinaryStringEncoding.Utf8;
                DataProtectionProvider provider = new DataProtectionProvide
                r("LOCAL=user");
                IBuffer message = CryptographicBuffer.ConvertStringToBinary
                (text, encoding);
                protectedData = await provider.ProtectAsync(message);
                plainTextBox.Text = "Protected data has " + protectedData.
                Length + " bytes";
                secureButton.Content = "Decrypt";
                plainTextBox.IsEnabled = false;
                encrypt = false;
            }
            else
            {
                BinaryStringEncoding encoding = BinaryStringEncoding.Utf8;
                DataProtectionProvider Provider = new DataProtectionProvider
                ("LOCAL=user");
```

```
                IBuffer unprotectedData = await Provider.
                UnprotectAsync(protectedData);
                plainTextBox.Text = CryptographicBuffer.
                ConvertBinaryToString(encoding, unprotectedData);
                secureButton.Content = "Encrypt";
                plainTextBox.IsEnabled = true;
                encrypt = true;
            }
        }
    }
}
```

Print and Casting Media to Devices

The PrintDocument class is used to handle interaction between your application and PrintManager. Again, let's trace back to the early days of computing and compare the difference between with and without this implementation. To print a document, you'd have to make a call to the particular printer with their individual API-the whole process. With this, all connected printers have been put under one roof: physically connected printers, wireless printers, cloud-connected printers, and even printing to a file format (PDF). All you need to do now is send your print call to this one place and all the available print options will open up.

As a user, when you click the Print button for any document (in Windows 10 or earlier), a pop-up asks you for printer choices, the number of copies to print, print options like color/grayscale, a preview window showing what the printed document will look like, and so on; when everything seems right to you, you send the document for your printer to print. In summary, the following steps are performed when printing a document:

1. Register your application for printing when the user clicks the Print button (you need to have a Print button in your UI).

2. Prepare the document for printing and send it to a preview window.

3. Unregister for printing when the operation is concluded.

Next, let's discuss how you can stream media (audio, video, images) to another device and how you can receive a media stream to your application. MediaPlayerElement already has a built-in casting button and implementation, so if you use it, you need not worry about doing anything else. But if you want to implement casting externally, you need to implement CastingDevicePicker from namespace Windows.Media.Casting. To cast media from to your remote devices, you need to

- Initialize your casting picker object.

- Add filters for the media type you wish to cast (audio, pictures, video).

- Add event handlers for casting.

Let's create an application to implement the two concepts. The output is shown in Figure 4-40.

Figure 4-40. *Printing on UWP*

XAML

```
<Page
    x:Class="PrintAndPlayToDemo.MainPage"
    xmlns="http://schemas.microsoft.com/winfx/2006/xaml/presentation"
    xmlns:x="http://schemas.microsoft.com/winfx/2006/xaml"
    xmlns:local="using:PrintAndPlayToDemo"
    xmlns:d="http://schemas.microsoft.com/expression/blend/2008"
    xmlns:mc="http://schemas.openxmlformats.org/markup-compatibility/2006"
    mc:Ignorable="d">
    <Grid Background="{ThemeResource ApplicationPageBackgroundThemeBrush}">
        <Grid.RowDefinitions>
            <RowDefinition/>
            <RowDefinition Height="120"/>
        </Grid.RowDefinitions>
        <Image x:Name="myPhoto" Margin="0" Source="Assets/myPhoto.JPG"/>
        <AppBarButton x:Name="printImage" Click="printImage_Click"
        HorizontalAlignment="Center" Icon="PreviewLink" Label="Print"
        Margin="0,0,100,0" Grid.Row="1" VerticalAlignment="Center"/>
        <AppBarButton x:Name="streamImage" Click="streamImage_Click"
        HorizontalAlignment="Center" Icon="SetTile" Label="Cast"
        Margin="100,0,0,0" Grid.Row="1" VerticalAlignment="Center"/>
    </Grid>
</Page>
```

C#

```
using System;
using Windows.Graphics.Printing;
using Windows.Media.Casting;
using Windows.UI.Xaml;
using Windows.UI.Xaml.Controls;
using Windows.UI.Xaml.Navigation;
using Windows.UI.Xaml.Printing;
namespace PrintAndPlayToDemo
{
    public sealed partial class MainPage : Page
    {
        private PrintDocument printDoc;
        private PrintManager printMan;
        private IPrintDocumentSource printDocSource;
        public MainPage()
        {
            this.InitializeComponent();
        }

        protected override void OnNavigatedTo(NavigationEventArgs e)
        {
            printMan = PrintManager.GetForCurrentView();
            printMan.PrintTaskRequested += PrintMan_PrintTaskRequested;
            printDoc = new PrintDocument();
            printDocSource = printDoc.DocumentSource;
            printDoc.Paginate += PrintDoc_Paginate;
            printDoc.GetPreviewPage += PrintDoc_GetPreviewPage;
            printDoc.AddPages += PrintDoc_AddPages;
        }
        //Printing
        private void PrintDoc_Paginate(object sender, PaginateEventArgs e)
        {
            printDoc.SetPreviewPageCount(1, PreviewPageCountType.Final);
        }
        private void PrintDoc_AddPages(object sender, AddPagesEventArgs e)
        {
            printDoc.AddPage(myPhoto);
            printDoc.AddPagesComplete();
        }
        private void PrintDoc_GetPreviewPage(object sender, GetPreviewPageEventArgs e)
        {
            printDoc.SetPreviewPage(e.PageNumber, myPhoto);
        }
        private void PrintMan_PrintTaskRequested(PrintManager sender,
        PrintTaskRequestedEventArgs args)
        {
```

```
    var printTask = args.Request.CreatePrintTask("Print",
    PrintTaskSourceRequested);
    printTask.Completed += PrintTask_Completed;
}
private void PrintTaskSourceRequested(PrintTaskSourceRequestedArgs args)
{
    args.SetSource(printDocSource);
}
private void PrintTask_Completed(PrintTask sender,
PrintTaskCompletedEventArgs args)
{
    //Notify user that printing has completed
}
private async void printImage_Click(object sender, RoutedEventArgs e)
{
    if (PrintManager.IsSupported())
    {
        await PrintManager.ShowPrintUIAsync();
    }
}
//Casting
CastingDevicePicker castingPicker;
private void streamImage_Click(object sender, RoutedEventArgs e)
{
    castingPicker = new CastingDevicePicker();
    castingPicker.Filter.SupportsPictures = true;
    if(castingPicker.Filter.SupportedCastingSources.Count == 0)
    {
        //no devices supported
    }
    castingPicker.CastingDeviceSelected += CastingPicker_
    CastingDeviceSelected;
}
private async void CastingPicker_CastingDeviceSelected(CastingDevice
Picker sender, CastingDeviceSelectedEventArgs args)
{
    await Dispatcher.RunAsync(Windows.UI.Core.
    CoreDispatcherPriority.Normal, async () =>
    {
        CastingConnection connection = args.SelectedCastingDevice.
        CreateCastingConnection();
        connection.ErrorOccurred += Connection_ErrorOccurred; ;
        connection.StateChanged += Connection_StateChanged; ;
        await connection.RequestStartCastingAsync(myPhoto.
        GetAsCastingSource());
    });
}
```

```
        private void Connection_StateChanged(CastingConnection sender, object args)
        {
            throw new NotImplementedException();
        }
        private void Connection_ErrorOccurred(CastingConnection sender,
        CastingConnectionErrorOccurredEventArgs args)
        {
            throw new NotImplementedException();
        }
    }
}
```

Windows Wheel Devices

This section will cover other devices that can be accommodated into your UWP
application, namely the Surface Dial introduced alongside Surface Studio. The
RadialController class accommodates wheel inputs for devices like the Surface Dial or
similar Windows Wheel devices. The syntax to initialize it is

```
RadialController myController = RadialController.CreateForCurrentView()
```

Further, menu items can be added to the radial controller using your own icons or
some of the known built-in icons, as shown in Figure 4-41.

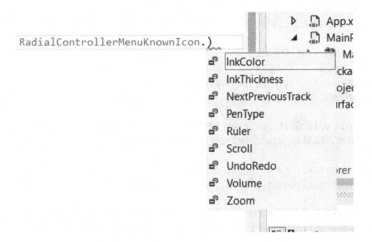

Figure 4-41. RadialController menu of known icons

C#

```csharp
using Windows.UI.Input;
using Windows.UI.Xaml.Controls;

namespace SurfaceDialDemo
{
    public sealed partial class MainPage : Page
    {
        RadialController myController;
        public MainPage()
        {
            this.InitializeComponent();
            if (RadialController.IsSupported()) //to check if it is
            supported on the machine
            {
                myController = RadialController.CreateForCurrentView();
                RadialControllerMenuItem newItem =
                RadialControllerMenuItem.CreateFromKnownIcon("Ink Color",
                RadialControllerMenuKnownIcon.InkColor);
                myController.Menu.Items.Add(newItem);
                myController.ButtonClicked += MyController_ButtonClicked;
                myController.RotationChanged += MyController_RotationChanged;
            }
        }

        private void MyController_RotationChanged(RadialController sender,
        RadialControllerRotationChangedEventArgs args)
        {
            double rotation = myController.RotationResolutionInDegrees;
            //Implement your code
        }

        private void MyController_ButtonClicked(RadialController sender,
        RadialControllerButtonClickedEventArgs args)
        {
            //Implement your code
        }
    }
}
```

Background Classes

Background classes are classes that keep running even after the user has exited the application. They are meant to run all the time. Background tasks are different from your UWP project and are added as a service reference. To add a background task, you need to create a Windows Runtime Component (Universal Windows) by right-clicking your solution and adding a new project. After you have done that, you need to add a reference to your UWP project prior to implementation.

The `IBackgroundTask` interface provides a method to work in the background. The background tasks are required to be lightweight for instance to update a live tile, for push notifications, to receive a mail or a message, or to play music in the background. Figure 4-42 shows the current background applications that are running on my machine.

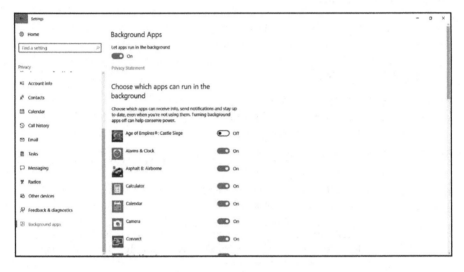

Figure 4-42. *Current background apps running*

In the previous chapter, you implemented an application and Cortana was able to activate the application to foreground and change the color theme. With a background application deep linked to Cortana, your application window need not open at all. A well-known example of this is your weather application. Asking "how's the weather today?" will cue Cortana to interact with the background application and display today's weather information inside Cortana's UI space. This is displayed in a *content card*. If you recall Windows 8/8.1 live tiles, they had to be done by a set of predefined templates. Similarly, at this stage Cortana provides four different templates for content cards. They are the following:

- Title only

- Title with up to three lines of text

- Title with image

- Title with image and up to three lines of text

Let's explore a background application before I talk about deep linking your background application with Cortana. The following example is from a piece of professional software that fetches the latest news feed as an article (the `Article` class was custom defined) and updates it to a live tile.

Here, I'd like you to take a moment to grasp the whole chapter. It is very important that you understand all the concepts laid out in this chapter to move ahead.

```csharp
using System;
using System.Collections.Generic;
using System.Linq;
using System.Net;
using System.Text;
using System.Threading.Tasks;
using System.Xml.Linq;
using Windows.ApplicationModel.Background;
using Windows.Data.Xml.Dom;
using Windows.Storage;
using Windows.UI.Notifications;

namespace BackgroundTaskLibrary
{
    public sealed class BackgroundTask : IBackgroundTask
    {
        List<Article> articles = new List<Article>();
        async void IBackgroundTask.Run(IBackgroundTaskInstance taskInstance)
        {
            BackgroundTaskDeferral deferral = taskInstance.GetDeferral();
            try
            {
                parseFeed();
                createLiveTile();
            }
            catch { }
        }

        public void createLiveTile()
        {
            articles = articles.Where(o => o.ImageUrl != null).ToList();
            TileUpdateManager.CreateTileUpdaterForApplication().Clear();
            TileUpdateManager.CreateTileUpdaterForApplication().
            EnableNotificationQueue(true);
            int count = 0;
            foreach (Article article in articles)
            {
                count++;
                XmlDocument squareTile = TileUpdateManager.GetTemplateConten
                t(TileTemplateType.TileSquarePeekImageAndText04);
                SetTextAndImage(squareTile, article);
                XmlDocument wideTile = TileUpdateManager.GetTemplateContent(
                TileTemplateType.TileWideSmallImageAndText03);
                SetTextAndImage(wideTile, article);
```

```
        IXmlNode visual = wideTile.ImportNode(squareTile.
        GetElementsByTagName("binding").Item(0), true);

        wideTile.GetElementsByTagName("visual").Item(0).
        AppendChild(visual);

        TileNotification tile = new TileNotification(wideTile);
        TileUpdateManager.CreateTileUpdaterForApplication().Update
        (tile);
        if (count == 5) break;
        tile.ExpirationTime = DateTime.Now.AddSeconds(3 * count);
    }
}

private static void SetTextAndImage(XmlDocument tileXml, Article article)
{
    XmlNodeList tileTextAttribute = tileXml.GetElementsByTagName
    ("text");
    tileTextAttribute[0].AppendChild(tileXml.CreateTextNode
    (article.Title));

    XmlNodeList tileImageAttributes = tileXml.GetElementsByTagName
    ("image");
    ((XmlElement)tileImageAttributes[0]).SetAttribute
    ("src", article.ImageUrl);
}

public void parseFeed()
{
    string url = "";
    string ned = ApplicationData.Current.RoamingSettings.
    Values["ned"].ToString();
    if (ApplicationData.Current.RoamingSettings.Values["FavoriteList"]
    != null)
    {
        string query = ApplicationData.Current.RoamingSettings.
        Values["FavoriteList"].ToString().Split('|')[0];
        url = "RSS uri here" + ned + "&q=" + query;
    }
    else
    {
        url = "Put your RSS uri here=" + ned;
    }

    XDocument rssFeed = XDocument.Load(url);
    var items = rssFeed.Root.Element("channel").Elements("item");

    foreach (XElement item in items)
    {
```

```
            Article objArticle = new Article();
            string description = item.Element("description").Value;

            HtmlDocument html = new HtmlDocument();
            html.LoadHtml(description);
            try
            {
                objArticle.ImageUrl = "http:" + html.DocumentNode.
                Descendants("img").ToList()[0].Attributes["src"].Value;
            }
            catch { }
            objArticle.Title = WebUtility.HtmlDecode(html.DocumentNode.
            Descendants("div").ToList().Single(o => o.Attributes[0].
            Value == "lh").Elements("a").ToList()[0].Element("b").
            InnerText);
            articles.Add(objArticle);
        }
    }
  }
}
```

By default, Cortana uses your 44x44 square logo from your manifest file. But you can include icons of sizes 68x68, 68x92, and 280x140 on a Cortana canvas. To activate a background app, you need to create a service application project under the same solution, as shown in Figure 4-43.

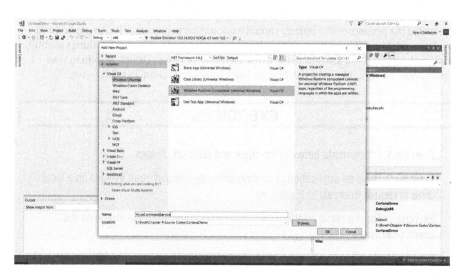

Figure 4-43. Creating a service application project

After you have done that, you need to add a reference to your original project and call the namespace to your service application. Implement the IBackgroundTask interface to your service application and add a Run method. The Run method is the entry point for Cortana into your background application. This is how you implement a background application with Cortana. Detailed documentation can be found at https://docs.microsoft.com/en-us/cortana/voicecommands/interact-with-a-background-app-in-cortana.

At this stage, we have covered quite a bit about Visual Studio and Blend, and how to design and implement different types of controls in our application. And I think this is the right time to talk a little bit about the Microsoft Fluent Design System introduced with Windows 10 Fall Creators Update in 2017. Fluent Design System adds some pretty controls to make the overall Windows experience a bit more tasteful and an opportunity for designers to make their Store apps more beautiful. And before getting into it, we are going to explore materials and textures. Textures are applied in one of 2 ways – from an image directly, or from one or more combination of mathematical equations (known as procedural texture) where even random noise in a material like a carpet is formed by equations. We know that Signature Type Cover on Surface Pro is advertised as two-tone style of Italian-made material known as Alcantara. If we were to develop a procedural texture of that two-tone material, we'd have different layers for different functions – one of which would be of the first color and the other of the second color. Other layers can be noise, blur, etcetera to give it the realistic visual feeling of the material as seen in real life. At the end, the API of that Alcantara texture would take in two colors as input for the desired color of Alcantara texture wherever implemented.

Fluent Design System introduces Acrylic material that's made of up 5 different layers – background of whatever is in behind the material, gaussian blur of the background, exclusion blend, a layer of color/tint, and finally a layer of noise texture. This should give you a hint that to apply this material, you need to pass in one single color as input. All the rest of the properties like opacity should work similar to any other Brush applied as a background. I hope I have been able to develop your intuition of how these things are built and implemented. You are now ready to use elements of Fluent Design System in your application using Acrylic material, Reveal, Motion and animation, Parallax, etcetera.

EXERCISES

Exercise 1: Differentiate between interface and abstract classes.

Exercise 2: Build an application to continuously capture and store images on a local drive at regular intervals until stopped.

Exercise 3: Build a photo capturing application and then store the image on the user's OneDrive.

Exercise 4: Continue exercise 3 and apply the globalization concept with Spanish and French.

Exercise 5: Associate yourself with APIs (like Bing APIs) and learn how to fetch images and data from XML/JSON structures.

CHAPTER 5

▪ ▪ ▪

Windows with Touch

The last chapter covered Windows app development with the mouse and keyboard and some of the related concepts. In this chapter, you'll take a step forward with touch.

Touch input adds a dimension to taking inputs from the user. It also suggests a reduction to the number of input choices from physical input devices such as a mouse and keyboard. What I mean is that with the introduction of a touch input keyboard (on-screen keyboard) you can make the number of keys and layout of the keys flexible depending on the current application.

In the early stages of learning about computing, you may have come across the information about input, process, and output shown in Figure 5-1. This is formally termed an input-process-output (IPO) model. And when the input and the output screens are the same, you have a touch screen. The IPO model of it is shown in Figure 5-2.

Figure 5-1. *Input-proces-output (IPO) model*

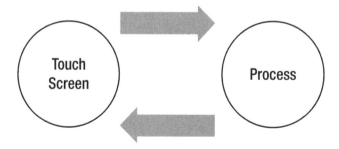

Figure 5-2. *IPO model for displays with touch inputs*

© Ayan Chatterjee 2017
A. Chatterjee, *Building Apps for the Universal Windows Platform*,
DOI 10.1007/978-1-4842-2629-2_5

Touch screens are just a subset of touch input devices. When we talk of a button or a switch, it's either pressed/turned on or not. But when we talk about touch, there are more variables attached to it than just pressed/turned on, namely the position of the touch. Further dimensions of input data are dependent on the touch input hardware in use: pressure, tilt, pen tip, and so on.

Gestures

Gestures are a fruitful outcome of touch inputs. They can be derived from a single touch to multi-touch. Gestures are a pattern/combination of touch inputs within a small duration of time. Previous chapters discussed in-built functions and custom-defined functions. Similarly, Windows provides us with some in-built touch gestures that are very common, such as tap and swipe. Figures 5-3 to 5-5 shows the gestures available in the Microsoft View 3D application first introduced with Windows 10 Creators Update.

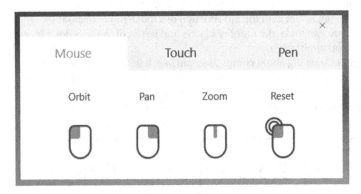

Figure 5-3. *View 3D mouse interactions*

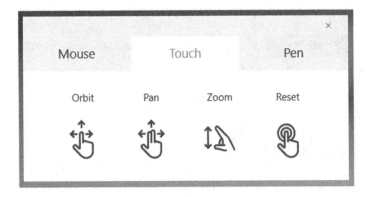

Figure 5-4. *View 3D touch interactions*

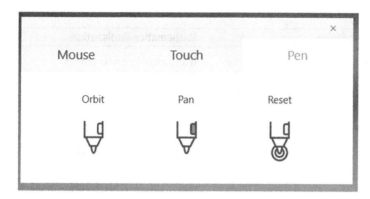

Figure 5-5. *View 3D pen interactions*

Touch gestures require movement on touch-enabled devices. Ideally, the movement can either be a function of space (in x-y directions), a function of pressure, a function of tilt with respect to the surface (such as pen inputs), a function of time (example: tap and hold), or combination of these factors depending on the touch input hardware. Some touch gestures are described in Table 5-1.

Table 5-1. *Basic Set of Touch Gestures*

Gesture	Description	Mathematics Explanation
Tap	One finger touches the screen and quickly lifts up.	Output: Position of touch (x, y).
Double tap	One finger performs two taps on the screen around the same area with a very minor time difference between both taps.	Output: Position of two touches $(x1, y1)$, $(x2, y2)$ where the distance and time difference between the points are within a predefined maximum allowed.
Two finger tap	Same as double tap, except that this is done by two different fingers, meaning the touch inputs occurred in different positions, at about the same time.	Output: Position of two touches $(x1, y1)$, $(x2, y2)$ where the distance is outside of a predefined surface area of a single point and the time difference between the points is within the predefined maximum allowed.
Press and hold	One finger touches the screen and stays for a while before lifting up.	Output: Position of touch (x, y), and position held for time > few milliseconds
Slide	One or more fingers touch the screen and move in the same direction.	If a straight line was drawn from end position (x_2, y_2) and start position (x_1, y_1), $R^2 \sim 1$.

(continued)

Table 5-1. (*continued*)

Gesture	Description	Mathematics Explanation
Swipe	One or more fingers touch the screen and move in the same direction for a short distance.	If a straight line was drawn from end position (x_2, y_2) and start position (x_1, y_1), $R^2 \sim 1$, and distance ~ few pixels.
Turn	Two fingers touch the screen and move in a clockwise or counter-clockwise direction.	Matrix/Array position points, where positions make up a circumference of a circle.
Pinch	Two fingers touch the screen and move closer to each other.	Matrix/Array for position points, where distance between positions keeps decreasing.
Stretch	Two fingers touch the screen and move apart.	Matrix/Array for position points, where distance between positions keeps increasing.

Gestures like tap, double tap, and right tap can be implemented inside XAML or C# (your preference) similar to how you implement the click of a button. To demonstrate this, let's create a simple application with a button and textbox, as shown in Figure 5-6. The XAML implementation is shown in Figure 5-7. The button listens for the three basic tap gestures and outputs on the textbox the action that has occurred, as shown in Figures 5-8 and 5-9.

Figure 5-6. *Application that listens for three basic gestures: tapped, double tapped, and right tapped*

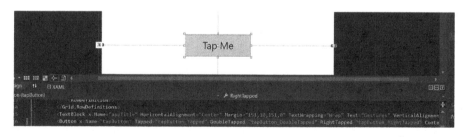

Figure 5-7. *XAML implementation of Figure 5-6*

Figure 5-8. *Response when a double tapped gesture has occurred*

Figure 5-9. *Response when a right tapped gesture has occurred*

You can create different types of combinations with simple touch gestures. If you have played a first-person shooter game, you have experience switching between normal view and the view through a scope of a gun via a right mouse-button click. You can do the same with RightTapped, while the firing of the weapon is done with left mouse button click or Click and Tapped events.

To use GestureRecognizer you need to declare the Windows.UI.XAML.Input namespace in your header. But why go through all the trouble to code basic gestures? The older generation of programmers may like coding because they have been trained to use MS-DOS and the command prompt, so typing lines of code seems familiar to them. But you are going to move forward and take advantage of Visual Studio. You are going to add another gesture to the program shown in Figure 5-6. The holding gesture will display how long a user has tapped and held the button. To do so, click the button and navigate to the event handling options (the lightning icon in the Properties section shown in Figure 5-10).

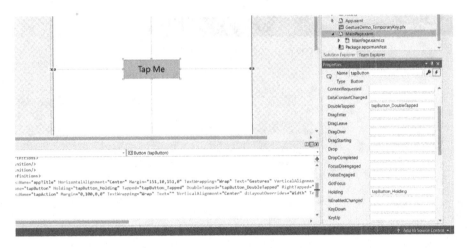

Figure 5-10. *Adding a Holding event listener to the program*

The C# implementation of holding for Figure 5-10 is

```
private void tapButton_Holding(object sender, HoldingRoutedEventArgs e)
{
        tapAction.Text = "Holding Event Triggered";
}
```

Defining a Custom Gesture

In the previous section, you learned to use in-built gestures. Here, you shall expand on that by building your own gesture. After you know how to define a custom gesture with a single touch input source (example: finger), it will be easier for you to work with multi-touch.

To define a custom gesture, you need to know the positions from the start of the touch input until the end of it. To explore how you can get and use touch input position points, let's make an example by placing a canvas on the application, as shown in Figure 5-11. ManipulationStarted tells you when a touch input manipulation has begun and will continue until the manipulation has exited or cancelled.

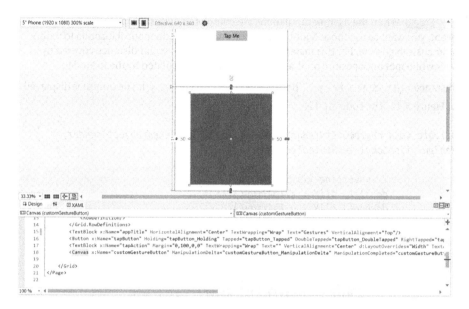

Figure 5-11. *Canvas implementation for custom gesture*

Note that in Figure 5-11, I've named the canvas as customGestureButton instead of naming it a canvas. Naming it canvas, although technically right and the compiler won't show any warning or error, will confuse a person later debugging or reading your code, so it's better to use a descriptive name.

Now let's execute touch inputs on the canvas step by step.

Step 1: You need variables to store X and Y positions. I have used a List of double datatypes to be more precise. You may choose another type depending on your requirements. The code for it is

```
List<double> x = new List<double>();
List<double> y = new List<double>();
```

Step 2: Now you must store the X and Y positions when the ManipulationDelta event is firing inside the canvas. The code for it is

```
private void customGestureButton_ManipulationDelta(object sender,
ManipulationDeltaRoutedEventArgs e)
{
        x.Add(e.Position.X);
        y.Add(e.Position.Y);
}
```

Step 3: When the user manipulations are completed in the ManipulationCompleted event, you want to use those X and Y positions and your mathematical formula to define your custom gesture. For this instance, I wish to display the scalar distance covered by a user while making a gesture on the canvas. Distance is calculated by the formula $distance = \sqrt{(x-x_1)^2 + (y-y_1)^2}$ between points (x, y) and (x₁, y₁). The output is displayed in Figure 5-12. The code for it is

```
private void customGestureButton_ManipulationCompleted(object sender,
ManipulationCompletedRoutedEventArgs e)
        {
            //Converting lists to array
            double[] allX = x.ToArray();
            double[] allY = y.ToArray();
            int length = x.Count;
            double distance = 0;
            for(int i = 2; i<length; i++)
            {
                distance += Math.Sqrt((Math.Pow(allX[i-1] - allX[i], 2)
                + Math.Pow(allY[i-1] - allY[i], 2)));
            }
            tapAction.Text = "Distance travelled is " + distance;

            //Clear All data to start a fresh gesture
            x.Clear();
            y.Clear();
}
```

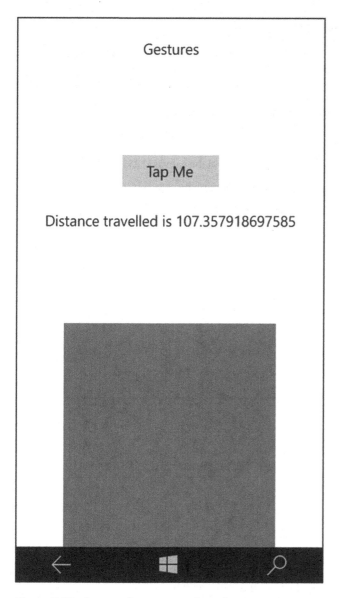

Figure 5-12. *Output when a gesture is made on canvas*

Working with Multi-Touch

When you receive more than one touch input positions at the same time, it means you are working with multi-touch. More than one input means more than one (x, y) coordinate position at the same time. What do we use when we have more than one of similar data? An array!

By now you are quite accustomed to RGB colors. To get three channels, you should have three dimensions of inputs. For this example application, you shall assign the following:

Red = (average of X positions / width of the canvas) * 255

Green = (average of Y positions / width of the canvas) * 255

Blue = (maximum Pythagorean distance in X and
Y / Pythagorean diagonal distance of the canvas) * 255

You are going to build a color picker using multi-touch. Figure 5-13 shows the front-end XAML part of the application.

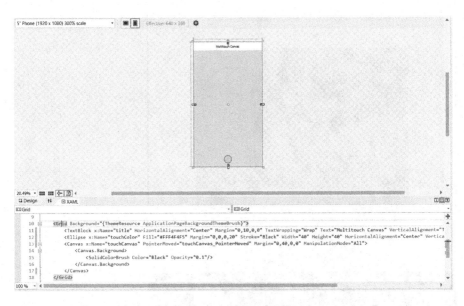

Figure 5-13. *Front end of multi-touch example application*

Similar to touch input from a single input pointer as seen in the previous section, the first step to using multi-touch is to know how many pointers are participating. To get this information, in this example, you will use

```
IList<PointerPoint> p = e.GetIntermediatePoints(touchCanvas);
```

The PointerPoint class is defined in Windows.UI.Input. Each individual input has its own identification, defined by PointerId, including input from the mouse pointer and the surface pen. If you are working with a specific device, you may want to filter out inputs from other PointerIds and you may want to filter out any PointerId duplicates in sensitive applications. Let's look at the C# implementation of your multi-touch example:

```
private void touchCanvas_PointerMoved(object sender, PointerRoutedEventArgs e)
    {
        IList<PointerPoint> p = e.GetIntermediatePoints(touchCanvas);
        int count = p.Count;
        double sumX = 0, sumY = 0, maxX = 0, maxY = 0;
        if(count >= 2)
        {
            for (int i = 0; i < count; i++)
            {
                PointerPoint current = p[i];
                sumX += current.Position.X;
                sumY += current.Position.Y;
                maxX = maxX < current.Position.X ?
                current.Position.X : maxX;
                maxY = maxY < current.Position.Y ?
                current.Position.Y : maxY;
            }
            double avgX = sumX / count;
            double avgY = sumY / count;
            byte R = Convert.ToByte(avgX * 255 / touchCanvas.
            ActualWidth);
            byte G = Convert.ToByte(avgY * 255 / touchCanvas.
            ActualHeight);
            byte B = Convert.ToByte(Math.Sqrt(Math.Pow(maxX, 2) + Math.
            Pow(maxY, 2)) / Math.Sqrt(Math.Pow(touchCanvas.ActualWidth,
            2) + Math.Pow(touchCanvas.ActualHeight, 2)));
            touchColor.Fill = new SolidColorBrush(Windows.UI.Color.
            FromArgb(255, R, G, B));

            title.Text = count.ToString() + " pointers";
        }
    }
```

Output from the multi-touch application is shown in Figure 5-14.

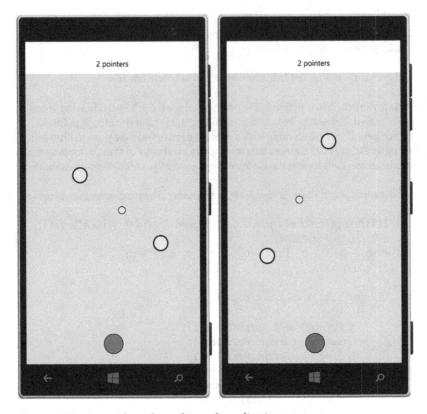

Figure 5-14. *Output from the multi-touch application*

EXERCISES

Exercise 1: Build a UWP application to import an image and use pinch and zoom to zoom in and out of the image.

Exercise 2: List the possible multi-touch gestures that come to your mind.

Exercise 3: Open the inking application you built previously and see what you can do with multi-touch.

Exercise 4: Build photo-editing software using multi-touch gestures.

CHAPTER 6

■ ■ ■

Internet of Things (IoT)

Before I talk about the Internet of Things, let's talk about responsibility: your responsibility as a developer and Microsoft's responsibility to provide the necessary tools. By now, you should know that application development requires four specific actors, which I'm referring to as makers, builders, tools, and the application. The makers are the architects and algorithm builders who design new concepts. The builders are the application developers who use a powerful IDE like Visual Studio to get the makers' work to a larger market. The tools are what the builder needs to quickly deliver those solutions, the application being the end product. It is your responsibility to build incredible solutions, keeping within the privacy and decency standards, while Microsoft's responsibility is to provide you the tools necessary to get the job done.

While the other chapters talk about how to use the hardware from a Windows PC, tablets, phones, cameras, and so on, with this chapter you move on to hardware beyond Windows devices. With IoT, you compile and use your own IoT hardware. Many of the things discussed here like Azure IoT Hub and Azure IoT Edge are still in preview as I am writing this chapter and things may be changed/improved, so I'll focus more on the theoretical aspects.

Let's take a moment to talk about the culture of this industry. We are in an industry that does not stick with the past or the present. The sooner we can make a model obsolete for something faster, more accurate, and improved, the better. This is great, and it demonstrates one's will to better oneself to reach new heights. If *old is gold*, we want to get something more valuable than gold; we struggle every single day to get to *priceless*!

Introduction

When you wish to work with more data and hardware other than your Windows device, you build an IoT application. Some examples of IoT applications are opening a garage door as soon as your car comes in front of it, automatically switching on and off the lights in your home, and so on. Or say you move from your study room to the kitchen to prepare for dinner, and the music system stops when you walk out of your study and goes with you as you walk to the kitchen. Or imagine a program for an university auditorium that senses how many people are inside in order to adjust the temperature of the room. The devices that participate in these scenarios make up the Internet of Things.

© Ayan Chatterjee 2017
A. Chatterjee, *Building Apps for the Universal Windows Platform*,
DOI 10.1007/978-1-4842-2629-2_6

A few decades ago, hardware was exclusive to big companies. As time went on, much like open source software, *open hardware* was put in place to make hardware available to everyone. However, programing for it then was incredibly complex. **Arduino** (an open source electronic prototyping platform) was invented to make it simple. This was a huge milestone in IoT history. The next notable milestone was the introduction of **Raspberry Pi**, which brought down the price of these devices to a wallet-friendly amount (less than $50).

Windows IoT is a baby version of Windows 10. To get started with IoT development, you will need a supported system on a chip (SoC). When you look at the differences between a computer in a traditional sense and a SoC, a computer has a monitor or a screen that displays some output, a keyboard and a mouse to get input, and a CPU. But a SoC can be anywhere, for instance collecting data autonomously in Antarctica, on a flight, in satellite, in military applications, and pushing the data in a cloud service like Azure to process the data for information.

A SoC may or may not have screens displaying information to users. It's completely your decision based on the application you will be making. A SoC without an output display is called *headless* and one with an output display is called *headed*.

Now let's talk a bit about an IoT dev (development) board. Figure 6-1 shows a Raspberry Pi IoT dev board. On first glance, you can see that there are a large number of pins poking out, ports you may or may not recognize, and some bumps on a rectangular shaped board. What do they do? These pins actually connect to various sensors and you can read/write data to and from these sensors. IoT dev boards are definitely nothing new in the world of computing but they are a growing market. The number of IoT dev boards in use is rapidly increasing today. Therefore, instead of going into a lot of programing in this chapter, I will focus more on what they are and how you can use them.

Figure 6-1. *Raspberry Pi IoT dev board*

The bumps are electronic components that are part of the board's circuit. If you wish to learn more about how these circuits are built, I suggest taking an electronics course to learn more about circuits, the associated physics, and components like transistors, capacitors, resistors, and diodes.

Windows 10 IoT Core

Now that you have purchased your IoT dev hardware, you need an operating system to run it. That operating system is Windows 10 IoT Core and it is the central command of the IoT.

Before talking more about Windows 10 IoT Core, let's discuss why you would want to use it compared to other options like Linux. I'll try to keep an unbiased opinion but here are some selling points:

- **Familiarity**

  Since you are reading this book and have read Chapters 1-5, I can assume you are well familiar with the Windows Universal Platform and the whole Windows ecosystem. The same continues with Windows 10 IoT Core—all the concepts of classes, structures, interface, and all of that C# syntax.

- **Simplicity**

  Writing your applications in a language like Visual C# is pretty high level. If you do not recall what a high level language is, it means it is closer to what we as people speak. Writing assembly-level code can be avoided using Windows 10 IoT Core.

  On top of that, Windows 10 IoT Core allows remote debugging. What does this mean? In your regular UWP project, before you debug, you need to select the architecture (ARM, x86 (32 bit), or x64 (64 bit)). Then you'll see a list of all connected devices that support the particular selected architecture including the local machine and even emulators for the architecture. After that, you click the green button to build and debug your application with breakpoints, line by line execution, or whatever it is that you prefer to do in the debugging process. The same concept carries over here. With remote debugging, first you need to enter your IoT device's IP and port number for successful communication to be established and then debug your application with similar breakpoints and however you prefer to debug your application.

- **Reusability**

   Most of the code you have written for your UWP application
   for desktop/mobile/holographic can be transferred to
   Windows 10 IoT Core depending on the capabilities. The
   inverse is also true. This means that it will be easier to write
   an IoT application if you already have an UWP project and it
   will be easier to create an UWP application if you have already
   built an IoT application.

To read/write data from all those different pins and sensors requires a different kind
of API that you do not need if you are building an UWP project for a tablet or a phone. You
do not have these kinds of pins poking out of your phone. To accommodate this change,
IoT extensions for UWP apps are required. One of the most commonly used is **GPIO
(General Purpose Input Output)**. GPIO is a generic pin that can be both an input and
an output depending on how you wish to use it. Think of it as a tiny USB drive where data
goes into your external hard drive and you can also read from your hard drive, but here it
can either read or write (one way) depending on how you want to use it.

To install Windows 10 IoT Core, you need to go to Windows Dashboard at
`https://developer.microsoft.com/en-us/windows/iot/GetStarted`, as shown in
Figure 6-2, select your board, and download and install Windows 10 IoT Core to the
microSD card you will use on your IoT dev board.

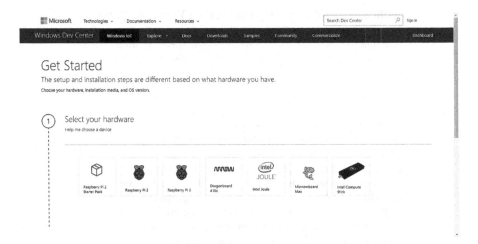

Figure 6-2. *Windows IoT on Windows Dev Ccenter*

To create an IoT application, you create a new UWP project and add the IoT
extension to get access to those IoT APIs shown in Figure 6-3. GPIO classes, structures,
and enums are managed under the `Windows.Devices.Gpio` namespace. Figures 6-4
and 6-5 show how you can use them. I think you can figure out how to program an IoT
application; it's like any other UWP application.

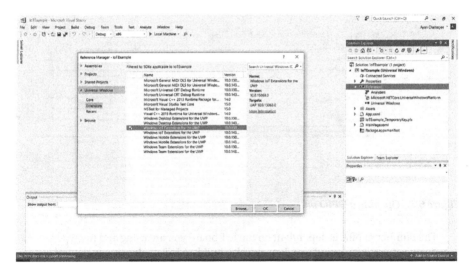

Figure 6-3. *Adding an IoT extension to your UWP project*

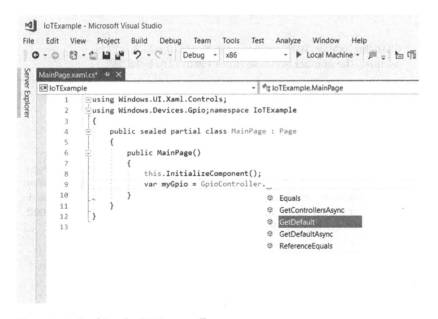

Figure 6-4. *Fetching the GPIO controller*

Figure 6-5. *Opening a GPIO pin*

The number of pins is dependent on the IoT board you are using and the type/ number of sensors connected to it. You can also build an IoT application to control/ manage other connected IoT devices.

Let's discuss data communication and how data is transferred. For binary data, the leftmost end is the *most significant bit (MSB)* and the rightmost end is the *least significant bit (LSB)*. Why are they called so? Let's consider the number 150, which in binary is 10010110.

Changing to MSB, 10010110 becomes 00010110, which is 22 in decimal. The number decreased from 150 to 22 or by 85.33%.

Changing to LSB, 10010110 becomes 10010111, which is 151 in decimal. The number increased from 150 to 151 or by 0.667%.

You can see that how an accidental change in MSB can affect the data a lot. The priority or significance of data increases from the leftmost to the rightmost bit. **Cyclic redundancy check (CRC)** is an algorithm put in place to detect such accidental changes to raw data being transferred. Data can be transferred in two ways: serial communication and parallel communication. Depending on your port, you can perform (connect to and transfer data) serial or parallel communication as necessary. If you have an IoT board, I think you are ready to build applications to run on it.

IoT on Microsoft Azure

In this section, I will talk about the range of services offered by Microsoft Azure. Of course, Microsoft Azure offers a lot of services and I can't cover everything in a single chapter so here I will focus on those most relevant to IoT. I've talked about things; now let's discuss some of the Internet part. Let's take the example of a traffic light controller.

Scenario 1: Without Sensor

The traffic lights turn on and off at a particular scheduled time (say every lane gets 5 minutes each). This gives cars in every lane a fair and equal amount of time. Even if traffic from one direction is heavy and it's light in the other direction, both lanes get equal time.

Scenario 2: IoT device with sensor but without Internet connectivity

Let's say a near-infrared camera is connected to your IoT board and you are making decisions to turn on/off traffic lights based on a direction's incoming traffic. The goal here is to get everyone moving quickly to wherever they need to go.

Scenario 3: IoT device with sensor and Internet connectivity

Scenario 2 is pretty good for day-to-day activity. But with Internet connectivity, you can connect your other IoT devices in a network. By joining the cloud-connected IoT, your traffic lights can be preprogrammed to change timing based on machine learning algorithms and the expected traffic in the next hour. On top of that, your IoT device can be prepared to handle unexpected situations like accidents, disasters, VIP traffic, and so on based on the design of your algorithm.

IoT Hub manages two-way communication from a device to a cloud service and from the cloud service back to the device. With IoT Hub, you can also authenticate your devices, manage connected devices, and perform other device management-related tasks. The Azure IoT suite offers a range of services within Microsoft Azure for your IoT devices. They are nothing you could not build yourself if you had the time to work on them. In summary, you could say Azure IoT Suite is a collection of the most widely used tasks. There are two main reasons why you need to collect data:

- **For analytics and action**

  Analytics is analysis of data like the number of users per day/week/month, the trend of use, the demographics of people using an application, etc. An *action* is doing something based on that data. Suppose your IoT device monitors the room lights. Lights need to be turned on and off when the owners are inside. But if your sensor detects some activity in your home when you are on holiday/in the office, the IoT device can alert the user or local authorities.

- **For machine learning**

  Machine learning algorithms can use your sensors' data in
  real time or over a long period of time depending on how
  computationally expensive your task is and the resources
  allocated to your learning algorithm. I will cover learning
  algorithms in Chapter 8, so for now, all you need to know is
  that you can collect raw data from your IoT device, implement
  a learning algorithm from the collected data, and make your
  IoT device more intelligent gradually over time. To explore the
  Azure IoT suite, visit `www.azureiotsuite.com/`.

Hitherto, I have covered the introductory details on Azure IoT Hub. However, not
all learning and fast decision making can occur in the cloud and this is where Azure
IoT Edge comes into play. Factories that use power tools and hazardous materials need
immediate responses, so the intelligence needs to run locally on the IoT devices. These
IoT devices executing intelligence locally are referred to as **IoT Edge** devices. Running
locally also means real-time decisions and low bandwidth costs. Azure IoT Edge uses
Azure IoT Hub for distribution of Microsoft's own and third-party services to IoT Edge
devices.

All of them are backed by a combination of Azure Stream Analytics, Azure Machine
Learning, Azure Functions, and Cognitive Services. With a lot of data from various
devices flowing in, you need a real-time, cost effective, and detailed insight of your data.
Azure Stream Analytics (`https://azure.microsoft.com/en-us/services/stream-analytics/`) does that. **Azure Machine Learning** (`https://azure.microsoft.com/en-us/services/machine-learning/`) offers a range of machine learning algorithms like
regression analysis, clustering, and anomaly detection, and Machine Learning Studio
provides a visual studio where you can use drag and drop to build your workflow. **Azure
Functions** (`https://azure.microsoft.com/en-us/services/functions/`) let you
quickly and easily run and test small pieces of your code directly from your web browser.
Cognitive Services (`https://azure.microsoft.com/en-us/services/cognitive-services/`) are a collection of intelligent algorithms like face detection, emotion
detection, and speech recognition presented as APIs for you to directly implement in your
application.

Microsoft Azure and all of these services discussed are proprietary to Microsoft and
to use them you need to have a subscription with Microsoft Azure. But why would you
want to use them? Let's discuss emotion detection in Cognitive Services as an example. If
you were to go on your own route, you would need to first filter out and extract faces using
some algorithm like Haar-like Feature and the Gabor Filter, and then you would need
to build your own emotion-detection algorithm using information from facial features,
which is brilliant if you wish to learn and research algorithms. It can also be time-consuming and has a risk of human error while building them. To avoid this and quickly
get to your solution, you can use all of these services.

Introduction to OpenCV

If you have a firm grasp of what has been covered, you have come a long way. I have talked about open hardware. Is there an open source collection of programs for various algorithms? OpenCV is a computer vision and machine learning software library. Even though OpenCV is older, like Azure IoT Suite, OpenCV consists of a collection of reusable algorithms related to computer vision. They are nothing that you could not build yourself if you had the time. Some of the common features that OpenCV incorporates are

- Image and video processing

- Object detection

- Face recognition

- Image reconstruction

- 3D modelling

- Image editing

- Object tracking

The list goes on and on. The reason I have only introduced and not gone into implementation with OpenCV is because of its depth of use and robustness in the world of image processing. However, as I author this chapter, there is no collection of NuGet packages for OpenCV, and incorporating them into IoT is incredibly complex. If you still wish to learn more about OpenCV, visit http://opencv.org/.

This chapter has been an introductory course into app development for the IoT. Now I recommend that you take the first step: connect your IoT device and start with the basics like making lights blink and building a line-following robot.

CHAPTER 7

Wearables

Previous chapters covered using Windows via the traditional mouse and keyboard combo, touch gestures, and the IoT. Now let's venture into wearable devices. Wearable devices are devices you wear everyday–on your wrist as in fitness bands or your head as in virtual, augmented, and mixed reality headsets. In other words, these devices attach to your body. You will first look into 3D and how 3D works. After you have learned the underlying principles and theories, we will discuss how to build holographic applications using Visual Studio.

A few decades ago, if you wore something like a virtual reality, augmented reality, or mixed reality headset and made pinching gestures on the street, people would have made a movie about you and named you an advanced alien robot. But now we can suit up and attach computers to our bodies. I don't think Charles Babbage or even the great Alan Turing imagined this possibility.

Microsoft HoloLens consists of several complex technologies and systems. It took several creative minds to build it. Before diving into HoloLens app development, however, let's take a moment to understand what 3D is and how it works.

3D

It is important to understand the difference between spatial data and spectral data. You will come across the term *spatial* while building HoloLens applications. Spatial data is the geometry or x-y-z data in space or a function of (x, y, z) in a Cartesian coordinate system. Spectral data refers to the function of a wavelength. To break it down into a much simpler explanation, for a spherical ball, the spatial data refers to its position in space and its shape containing a surface area of $4\pi r^2$ where r is its radius. Spectral data are the digital numbers emitted by the ball for different wavelengths (RGB for us) making it a red ball or a blue ball or an orange ball.

If you remember the elementary aspects of 3D, a line is made by two points in space. Three points or three lines make a surface in space (Figure 7-1). The surface has a normal vector to know which side is pointing outward and which one is inward. So, for a closed body (3D box) with height of 10, width of 5, depth of 2, and starting from (0, 0, 0) in a triangular mesh, the data is as shown in Figure 7-2 and Table 7-1.

© Ayan Chatterjee 2017
A. Chatterjee, *Building Apps for the Universal Windows Platform*,
DOI 10.1007/978-1-4842-2629-2_7

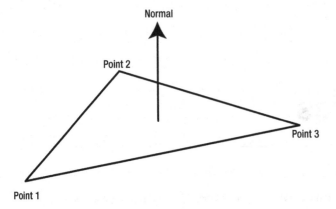

Figure 7-1. *A triangular flat surface in space*

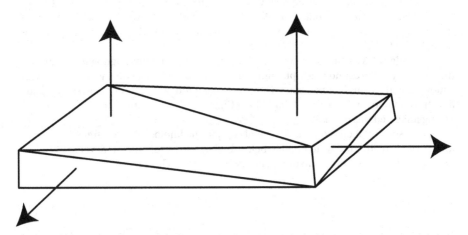

Figure 7-2. *Triangular mesh of a 3D box*

Table 7-1. *Triangular Mesh Data of a 3D Box*

Points	Normal
(0, 0, 2), (0, 10, 2), (5, 0, 2)	Up
(0, 10, 2), (5, 0, 2), (5, 10, 2)	Up
(0, 0, 0), (0, 0, 2), (0, 10, 2)	Side 1 (say right)
(0, 0, 0), (0, 0, 2), (0, 10, 0)	Side 1 (say right)
(0, 0, 0), (0, 0, 2), (0, 10, 2)	Side 2
(0, 0, 0), (0, 0, 2), (0, 10, 0)	Side 2
(0, 0, 0), (5, 0, 2), (5, 10, 2)	Side 3
(0, 0, 0), (5, 0, 2), (5, 10, 0)	Side 3
(0, 0, 0), (5, 0, 2), (5, 0, 0)	Side 4
(0, 0, 2), (5, 0, 2), (5, 0, 0)	Side 4
(0, 0, 0), (0, 10, 0), (5, 0, 0)	Down
(0, 10, 0), (5, 0, 0), (5, 10, 0)	Down

3D applications are built using this concept. File types like Wavefront Object (OBJ) and others all store 3D model data in this way. In the real world, when a light source emits radiance in different wavelengths, it is joined in with others emitted by other light sources. That light travels through the atmosphere, and some of it is absorbed depending on the concentration of gasses present in that particular region of the atmosphere at that time. The remaining ones fall on a body (spatial data). Light then reflects, refracts, and scatters, and the reflected light goes up to the atmosphere to be captured by a camera in digital form or for our own eyes to see (spectral data).

What a 3D scene consists of is the environment (background and atmosphere), players (objects in the scene), and an observer (camera or eye). Figure 7-3 shows a window in Microsoft's Paint 3D, released with Windows 10 Creators Update; Figure 7-4 shows a window in SolidWorks, an application used by a lot of engineers; and Figure 7-5 shows a window in Autodesk Maya, which is used by several animators. They are three examples of a 3D modelling application.

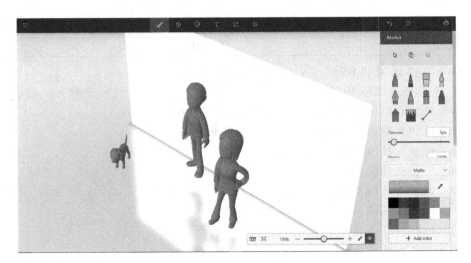

Figure 7-3. *Microsoft Paint 3D*

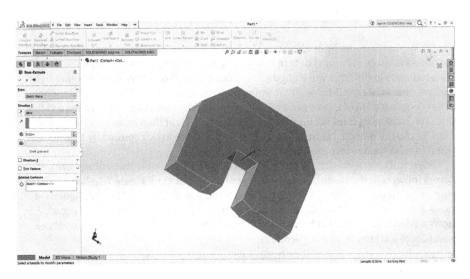

Figure 7-4. *SolidWorks*

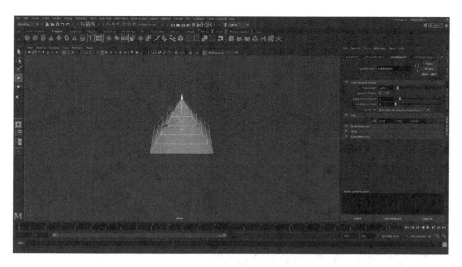

Figure 7-5. *Autodesk Maya*

The underlying physics and mathematics of these major applications and any other developed in the future will remain the same. They are also used in the robotics industry.

A player or object is made up of a several mathematical equations. It may be a single polygon or a complex combination of several polygons. They have materials and physical properties. They can move in space, so for motion they will have some roll, pitch, and yaw values for angular motion and x, y, and z directions for movement. Light sources have intensity (how bright it is), position (where the light source is), elevation (how high it is from the ground), and azimuth angle (the direction the light source is pointing to). The camera or observer will also have a position, elevation, and azimuth angle. The angle(s) will differ depending on whether it is a point light source, directional light source, or some other. In a point source of light, the rays of light emit from one single point in space. Similarly, a directional light source produces light rays coming in parallel from one direction. In a nutshell, it represents the size and shape of the light-emitting object. An advanced user may create an incredibly complex shape emitting light but for the purposes of this book, you'll stick to the basics. The observer or camera will have some properties for realistic rendering such as aperture, shutter speed, ISO, and so on. Let's verify this with a screenshot from Windows Holographic application shown in Figure 7-6.

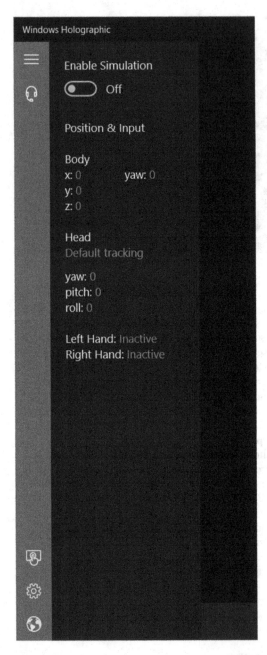

Figure 7-6. *Information shown in the Windows Holographic application*

Rendering is creating a 2D image from 3D. It is basically ray tracing from sources of light in the scene and it'll look pixel by pixel based on several factors such as the object's material properties, reflection, refraction, scattering, angle between source of light and object as seen from the camera causing a Lambertian reflectance, and so on. It works like this: light rays are first fired into space from light-emitting objects (the light source). Sampling algorithms play a role here to select only a few light rays because you need to think about the computational capabilities of your device. The light rays then strike the 3D objects and bounce back according to its material properties. The bounced-back light comes to a sensor (camera) and you see the image formed on a screen (in this case, a holographic device display). The more details you have about the physics of the scene and the objects in it, the more realistic your rendering output, if you have the time to render in detail.

Real Time

Real time occurs when there is no time difference between an action and a response. To achieve true real time, the algorithm and the data needs to be ready even before the user has pressed a button or created an action. What we look for is *near real time*, which is close to the time it takes for eyelids to flicker. We wish to make our program run fast enough that a user does not feel a sense of delay or even knows if something is processing (i.e. $\Delta t \sim 0$). This near real-time experience makes a big difference in applications. When working with UWP, especially HoloLens applications, test your application before deploying it to the Store.

A deadline is the time when a program is expected to finish. There are three types of real-time deadlines: hard, firm, and soft. Hard deadlines are the deadlines that, when missed, create a total system failure; firm deadlines when missed are sometimes tolerable; and missing a soft deadline results in a decline in the quality of service. In other words, missing a soft, firm, and hard deadline results in not good, disastrous, and catastrophic outcomes, respectively.

Developing For Microsoft HoloLens

To develop for HoloLens, the tools you need are Visual Studio with Windows 10 SDK, HoloLens Emulator or the actual device, and Unity for 3D modelling. To clarify, Microsoft HoloLens is the device by Microsoft among other devices from hardware manufacturers employing Windows Holographic. Detailed documentation can be found at Microsoft's official HoloLens website at https://developer.microsoft.com/windows/holographic. Now that you know what 3D is, you can develop for Microsoft HoloLens with ease. Creating a new project is the same as creating a new UWP application (after all, the whole point of UWP is to have everything in one solution). Adding HoloLens or any other Virtual Reality headset can be added from the devices section in Windows Settings. Then you follow the Windows Holographic application to set it up, as shown in Figures 7-7 through 7-9. Note that Figure 7-8 requests the height of the person using it. These screenshot images may look different on your machine by the time you read this book due to UI and other changes. If you recall, in the 3D section, we talked about position, elevation, azimuth angle, and where it is used.

Figure 7-7. Preparing a room for wearable headsets in Windows Holographic

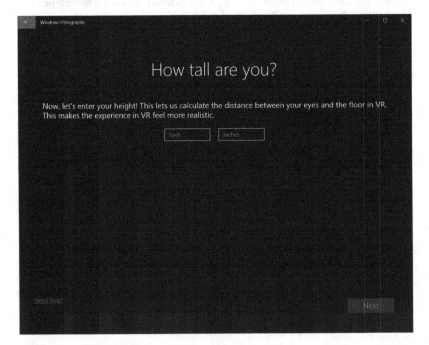

Figure 7-8. Elevation of observer request in Windows Holographic

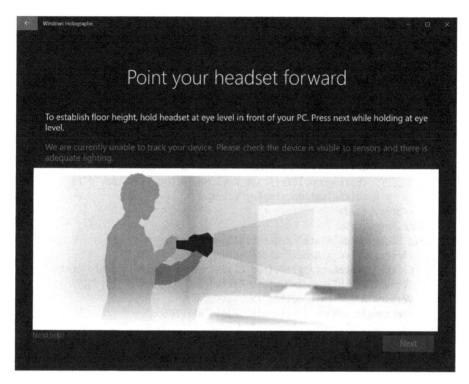

Figure 7-9. Setting up the room in Windows Holographic

With regular apps, you move the mouse pointer to navigate the GUI. With touch, you make contact with the touch screen and (x, y) position points are sent accordingly. And with HoloLens, navigation on the screen is done by tracking the person's head movement. With a mouse, click events are fired by left and right clicks. With touch, it is taps and gestures. And with HoloLens, it is called air tap and it is a gesture the user makes by pinching in the air (bringing two fingers closer to one another). You can take a closer look at the gestures at the Microsoft support site at `https://support.microsoft.com/en-in/help/12644/hololens-use-gestures`.

The bloom gesture opens the Start menu in HoloLens. Gaze is the holographic display replacement for the mouse. Gaze will allow you to click buttons and move objects and holograms in that holographic space. Air tap is for selection. The gaze and other gesture inputs in Microsoft HoloLens are converted into touch events. So, if your app is built for touch inputs, you are already good to go with a 2D holographic application. You do not need Unity 3D for a 2D holographic application. Let's create a simple UWP application like you normally do with a storyboard animation and see how it plays out on HoloLens. The XAML and C# for it are as follows:

XAML

```
<Page
    x:Class="HolographicDemo.MainPage"
    xmlns="http://schemas.microsoft.com/winfx/2006/xaml/presentation"
    xmlns:x="http://schemas.microsoft.com/winfx/2006/xaml"
```

```xml
    xmlns:local="using:HolographicDemo"
    xmlns:d="http://schemas.microsoft.com/expression/blend/2008"
    xmlns:mc="http://schemas.openxmlformats.org/markup-compatibility/2006"
    mc:Ignorable="d">
    <Page.Resources>
        <Storyboard x:Name="RotateRectangle" AutoReverse="True"
        RepeatBehavior="Forever">
            <DoubleAnimationUsingKeyFrames EnableDependentAnimation="True"
            Storyboard.TargetProperty="(FrameworkElement.Width)" Storyboard.
            TargetName="rectangle">
                <EasingDoubleKeyFrame KeyTime="0" Value="100"/>
                <EasingDoubleKeyFrame KeyTime="0:0:0.5" Value="0"/>
            </DoubleAnimationUsingKeyFrames>
        </Storyboard>
    </Page.Resources>
    <Grid Background="Black" RequestedTheme="Dark">
        <AppBarButton x:Name="rotateRectangleButton"
        Click="rotateRectangleButton_Click" HorizontalAlignment="Center"
        Icon="Refresh" Label="Rotate Rectangle" Margin="0,0,0,100"
        VerticalAlignment="Bottom"/>
        <Rectangle x:Name="rectangle" Fill="#FFFF0606"
        HorizontalAlignment="Center" Height="100" Margin="0,0,0,100"
        Stroke="White" VerticalAlignment="Center" Width="100"
        StrokeThickness="4"/>
    </Grid>
</Page>
```

C#

```csharp
using System;
using Windows.UI.Xaml;
using Windows.UI.Xaml.Controls;

namespace HolographicDemo
{
    public sealed partial class MainPage : Page
    {
        public MainPage()
        {
            this.InitializeComponent();
        }

        private Boolean rectangleRotating { get; set; } = false;

        private void rotateRectangleButton_Click(object sender,
        RoutedEventArgs e)
        {
```

```
        if (rectangleRotating)
        {
            RotateRectangle.Stop();
            rotateRectangleButton.Label = "Rotate Again";
            rectangleRotating = false;
        }
        else
        {
            RotateRectangle.Begin();
            rotateRectangleButton.Label = "Stop Rotation";
            rectangleRotating = true;
        }
    }
  }
}
```

It is a simple and straightforward application. Figure 7-10 shows how it looks on a normal Windows 10 desktop or laptop and Figure 7-11 shows how it appears on a HoloLens emulator.

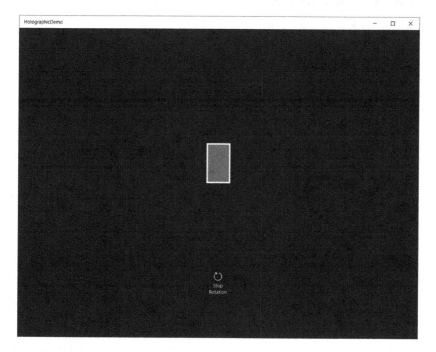

Figure 7-10. *Simple UWP application*

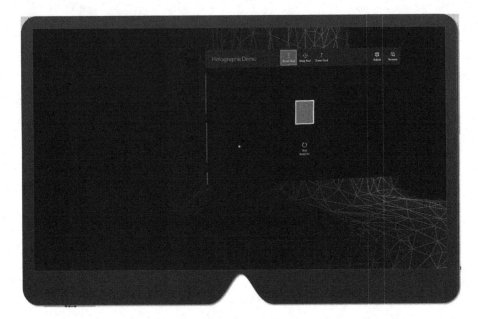

Figure 7-11. *2D UWP Holographic application*

Voila! You can now prepare your UWP app for Microsoft HoloLens. For 3D, Unity 3D is the preferred application. To install Unity, simply download and install it from the website along with Windows Store components, as shown in Figure 7-12. By now, installations and the creation of new projects should be pretty familiar. Be sure to create a 3D project for HoloLens, as shown in Figure 7-13.

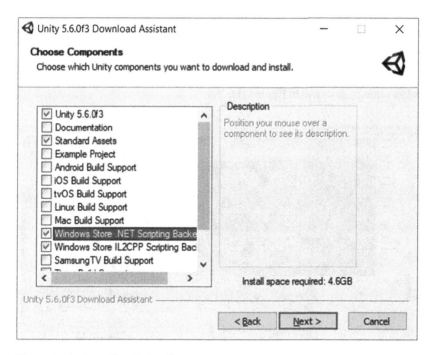

Figure 7-12. *Installing Unity 3D*

Figure 7-13. *Creating a new Unity 3D project*

On creation of a new project, a couple of things need to be kept in mind. One of them is spatial mapping. I have discussed what spatial dimension is, and you need to map the environment to do things like place a 3D model like a cartoon character on a piece of furniture. Without mapping the 3D environment (room) you'd be guessing the position and might end up placing the object in an unrealistic way. To do this, you need to enable it from project settings, as shown in Figure 7-14.

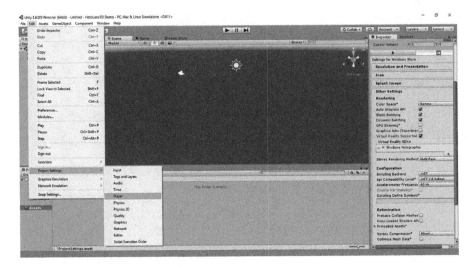

Figure 7-14. *Adjusting player settings for HoloLens*

Some common settings and preferences to be kept in mind are the following:

- Enable Windows Holographic under Virtual Reality SDK in Player Settings.

- Enable device capabilities such as microphone and InternetClientServer under Publishing Settings in Player Settings.

- Change quality settings from Fantastic to Fastest under Quality Settings. This is hardware dependent and a personal call depending on whether your application is computationally expensive.

- Center the camera position and set clear flags to solid color black. HoloLens considers black as transparent and if this is not done, then the user won't be able to see the environment.

- Set build settings to Windows 10 and UWP SDK to D3D and export your Visual Studio project, as shown in Figure 7-15. Exporting Unity C# Projects in Build Settings will export for Visual Studio and enable IntelliSense in your application.

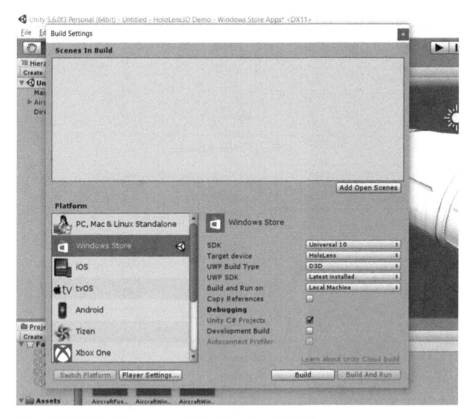

Figure 7-15. *Unity 3D recommended build settings for HoloLens*

You are now ready to build your scenes for Windows Holographic if you are familiar with 3D modelling and basically familiar with Unity 3D. If not, I suggest that you learn how to use Unity 3D first.

Deployment and Store Ready

Deploying HoloLens apps to the store is pretty straightforward. The first step, as with a Windows Universal solution, is to create app packages for the store. This is shown in Figures 7-16 and 7-17.

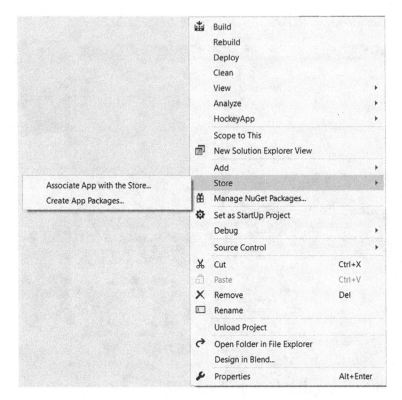

Figure 7-16. *Right-click the UWP project to initiate app package creation*

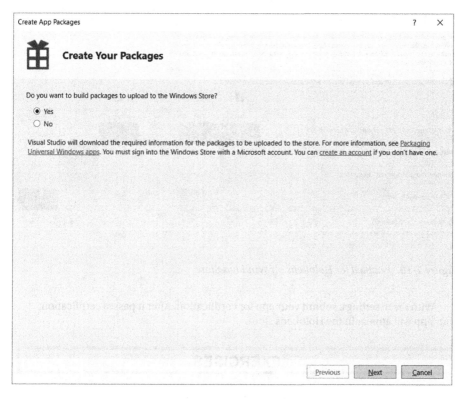

Figure 7-17. *Building a package for the Store*

Next, upload your package to your application's dashboard on the Windows Store developer dashboard. When you upload it, your UWP app that supports HoloLens will be ticked. If unticked, check the checkbox and save. You should see everything as displayed in Figure 7-18.

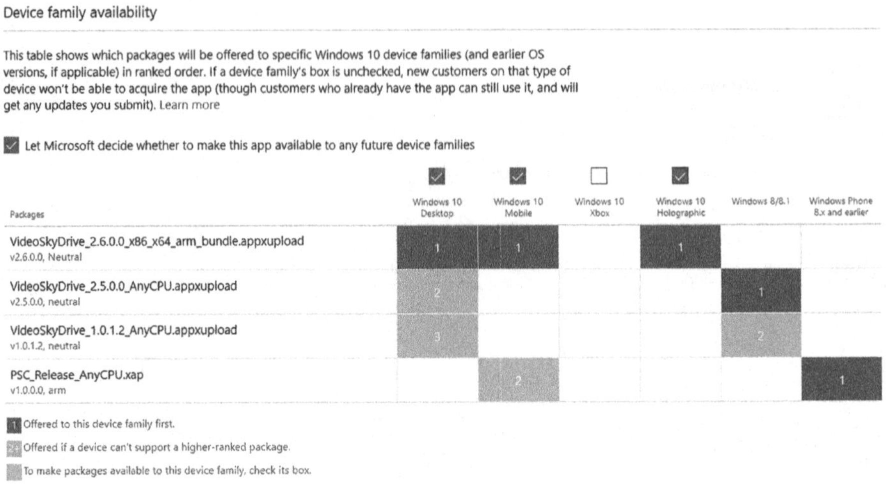

Device family availability

This table shows which packages will be offered to specific Windows 10 device families (and earlier OS versions, if applicable) in ranked order. If a device family's box is unchecked, new customers on that type of device won't be able to acquire the app (though customers who already have the app can still use it, and will get any updates you submit). Learn more

☑ Let Microsoft decide whether to make this app available to any future device families

Packages	Windows 10 Desktop	Windows 10 Mobile	Windows 10 Xbox	Windows 10 Holographic	Windows 8/8.1	Windows Phone 8.x and earlier
	☑	☑	☐	☑		
VideoSkyDrive_2.6.0.0_x86_x64_arm_bundle.appxupload v2.6.0.0, Neutral	1	1		1		
VideoSkyDrive_2.5.0.0_AnyCPU.appxupload v2.5.0.0, neutral	2				1	
VideoSkyDrive_1.0.1.2_AnyCPU.appxupload v1.0.1.2, neutral	3				2	
PSC_Release_AnyCPU.xap v1.0.0.0, arm		2				1

1 Offered to this device family first.
2 Offered if a device can't support a higher-ranked package.
▓ To make packages available to this device family, check its box.

Figure 7-18. *Enabled for HoloLens on Windows Store*

With these settings, submit your app for certification. After it passes certification, your app will appear in the HoloLens store.

EXERCISES

Exercise 1: Take one of your favorite applications you have built, and optimize the 2D application layout for a better Holographic experience.

Exercise 2: Build a basic 3D Windows Holographic application to implement audio playing from one point in space.

Exercise 3: Build a 3D Windows Holographic application of your favorite cartoon character and make it follow you around, jumping on objects on its path.

CHAPTER 8

■ ■ ■

Windows 10 for Advanced Users

This will be a bit different but please bear with this paragraph. Imagine monkeys living in a mostly unexplored forest where some trees are thicker and more comfortable to live in than others. Scientist/explorer monkeys take the first jump into the unknown parts of the forest in search of the thickest and most comfortable tree in the forest. Each team of scientist monkeys has their own heading or direction of exploration–some search by a planned route and some search via accidental luck. And whenever these scientist monkeys find a tree more comfortable than the present tree where all the other monkeys are, the scientist monkeys pass the information to the developer monkeys. It's the job of the developer monkeys to make a smooth transition for the other monkeys to follow from the current tree to the more comfortable one.

In real life, researchers and scientists invent something new, and their job is to make their hypothesis work correctly, no matter how much time it takes. But developers have a responsibility to make their program fast and responsive enough to be distributed to the general public. In this chapter, you will learn some of the advanced concepts of Windows 10.

Inking

Inking or pen inputs have taken a major place among the public, especially with the Microsoft Surface brand of Windows devices. Before the arrival of the Windows 10 Anniversary update, many major applications used *Canvas* as their inking playground. Every touch input to *Canvas* was handled by the ManipulationDelta method. But recently *InkCanvas* has taken the lead when it comes to inking. For the first example, you shall build a simple inking application. InkCanvas and InkToolbar controls have been placed on the screen, as shown in Figure 8-1; the application is shown in Figure 8-2.

© Ayan Chatterjee 2017
A. Chatterjee, *Building Apps for the Universal Windows Platform*,
DOI 10.1007/978-1-4842-2629-2_8

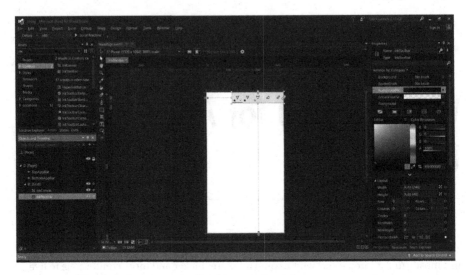

Figure 8-1. *Blend window for a simple inking application*

Figure 8-2. *Simple inking application*

The XAML and code behind for this app follows:

XAML

```
<Page
    x:Class="Inking.MainPage"
    xmlns="http://schemas.microsoft.com/winfx/2006/xaml/presentation"
    xmlns:x="http://schemas.microsoft.com/winfx/2006/xaml"
    xmlns:local="using:Inking"
    xmlns:d="http://schemas.microsoft.com/expression/blend/2008"
    xmlns:mc="http://schemas.openxmlformats.org/markup-compatibility/2006"
    mc:Ignorable="d">

    <Grid Background="{ThemeResource ApplicationPageBackgroundThemeBrush}">
        <InkCanvas x:Name="inkCanvas" Margin="0"/>
        <InkToolbar x:Name="inkToolbar" TargetInkCanvas="{x:Bind inkCanvas}"
        Margin="0" VerticalAlignment="Top" d:LayoutOverrides="Width"
        HorizontalAlignment="Right"/>
    </Grid>
</Page>
```

C#

```
using Windows.UI.Core;
using Windows.UI.Xaml.Controls;

namespace Inking
{
    public sealed partial class MainPage : Page
    {
        public MainPage()
        {
            this.InitializeComponent();
            inkCanvas.InkPresenter.InputDeviceTypes = CoreInputDeviceTypes.
            Pen | CoreInputDeviceTypes.Touch | CoreInputDeviceTypes.Mouse;
        }
    }
}
```

This is all you need to create a basic inking application. For those of you using previous versions of Visual Studio, you need to install the InkToolbar control separately and add a reference to it in your Visual Studio Project to make it work. For those using Visual Studio 2017, you need not worry about it.

Device-Specific Code

While the general idea of a universal platform makes things easier, each category of device is unique. Mobile and ARM processors are designed for lightweight, low energy applications. PCs and laptops can perform computationally expensive tasks. Similarly, in your application you may want to write some device-specific code to make the most of every device.

This can be achieved in two ways:

1. DeviceFamily-Type folder

2. DeviceFamily-Type file name

If you recall the scalable assets sections, you can use different optical scaling of the same asset with

```
filename.scale-scalefactor.extension
```

Similarly, you can target several device families in UWP with

```
filename.DeviceFamily-type.extension
```

Presently, the device families available in Windows Universal are

- Universal device family

- Desktop device family

- Mobile device family

- IoT device family

- Xbox Live device family

For the demonstration, you shall be doing it in code behind by creating two XAML pages and naming them `MainPageDesktop` and `MainPageMobile` for desktop and mobile devices, respectively. The output is shown in Figure 8-3. Personally, I recommend implementing this in the code behind because I find it is easier to customize when trying to implement Windows 10 devices and version-specific layouts, or a change like an implementation of a new UI for a page for a specific device family. Reverting to the old version of the page is easier if an error occurs with the new page during runtime.

XAML (MainPageDesktop)

```
<Page
    x:Class="DeviceSpecificDemo.MainPageDesktop"
    xmlns="http://schemas.microsoft.com/winfx/2006/xaml/presentation"
    xmlns:x="http://schemas.microsoft.com/winfx/2006/xaml"
    xmlns:local="using:DeviceSpecificDemo"
    xmlns:d="http://schemas.microsoft.com/expression/blend/2008"
    xmlns:mc="http://schemas.openxmlformats.org/markup-compatibility/2006"
    mc:Ignorable="d">
```

```
<Grid Background="{ThemeResource ApplicationPageBackgroundThemeBrush}">
    <TextBlock Text="This is the Desktop version"
    HorizontalAlignment="Center" VerticalAlignment="Bottom"
    Margin="0,0,0,100" FontSize="20"/>
    <Image Margin="0,100,0,150" Source="Assets/surfaceStudio.jpg"
    Stretch="Uniform"/>
</Grid>
</Page>
```

XAML (MainPageMobile)

```
<Page
    x:Class="DeviceSpecificDemo.MainPageMobile"
    xmlns="http://schemas.microsoft.com/winfx/2006/xaml/presentation"
    xmlns:x="http://schemas.microsoft.com/winfx/2006/xaml"
    xmlns:local="using:DeviceSpecificDemo"
    xmlns:d="http://schemas.microsoft.com/expression/blend/2008"
    xmlns:mc="http://schemas.openxmlformats.org/markup-compatibility/2006"
    mc:Ignorable="d">
    <Grid Background="{ThemeResource ApplicationPageBackgroundThemeBrush}">
        <TextBlock Text="This is the mobile version"
        HorizontalAlignment="Center" Margin="0,120,0,0"/>
        <Image Margin="0" Source="Assets/windowsPhone.jpg" Stretch="Uniform"
        VerticalAlignment="Bottom"/>
    </Grid>
</Page>
```

App.xaml.cs

```
using System;
using Windows.ApplicationModel;
using Windows.ApplicationModel.Activation;
using Windows.UI.Xaml;
using Windows.UI.Xaml.Controls;
using Windows.UI.Xaml.Navigation;
namespace DeviceSpecificDemo
{
    sealed partial class App : Application
    {
        public App()
        {
            this.InitializeComponent();
            this.Suspending += OnSuspending;
        }
        protected override void OnLaunched(LaunchActivatedEventArgs e)
        {
```

```
        Frame rootFrame = Window.Current.Content as Frame;
        if (rootFrame == null)
        {
            rootFrame = new Frame();

            rootFrame.NavigationFailed += OnNavigationFailed;

            if (e.PreviousExecutionState == ApplicationExecutionState.
            Terminated)
            {
                //TODO: Load state from previously suspended application
            }
            Window.Current.Content = rootFrame;
        }

        if (e.PrelaunchActivated == false)
        {
            if (rootFrame.Content == null)
            {
                switch (Windows.System.Profile.AnalyticsInfo.
                VersionInfo.DeviceFamily)
                {
                    case "Windows.Desktop": //For Desktop Family
                        rootFrame.Navigate(typeof(MainPageDesktop),
                        e.Arguments);
                        break;
                    case "Windows.Mobile": //For Mobile Family
                        rootFrame.Navigate(typeof(MainPageMobile),
                        e.Arguments);
                        break;
                    default:
                        //It is recommended to put a default in-case of
                        failure to detect device family or connected to
                        any other device family
                        break;
                }
            }
            // Ensure the current window is active
            Window.Current.Activate();
        }
    }
    void OnNavigationFailed(object sender, NavigationFailedEventArgs e)
    {
        throw new Exception("Failed to load Page " + e.SourcePageType.
        FullName);
    }
```

```
        private void OnSuspending(object sender, SuspendingEventArgs e)
        {
            var deferral = e.SuspendingOperation.GetDeferral();
            deferral.Complete();
        }
    }
}
```

Figure 8-3. *Output of DeviceSpecificDemo application*

App Protocols

When you type a web address in a browser, you start with http or https, which is the hypertext transfer protocol and the s in https stands for *secure*. This is a protocol or set of rules that governs the transfer of hypertext, be it a static or dynamic web page. Other than that, *mailto* launches the default mail application with given parameters, *tel* makes a phone call with default phone calling client application, and so on.

Apps can also contain protocols. For this example, you shall build a demo application to call a Skype URI, as shown in Figures 8-4 and 8-5.

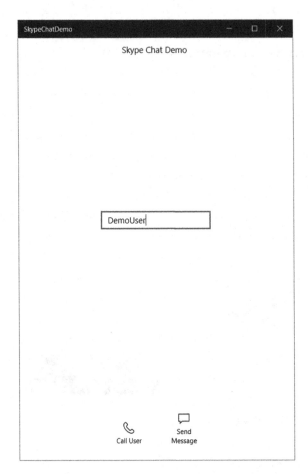

Figure 8-4. Skype URI demo application

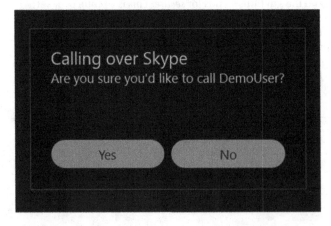

Figure 8-5. Response from Skype when the call button is pressed

The XAML and C# code for the application follow:

XAML

```xml
<Page
    x:Class="SkypeChatDemo.MainPage"
    xmlns="http://schemas.microsoft.com/winfx/2006/xaml/presentation"
    xmlns:x="http://schemas.microsoft.com/winfx/2006/xaml"
    xmlns:local="using:SkypeChatDemo"
    xmlns:d="http://schemas.microsoft.com/expression/blend/2008"
    xmlns:mc="http://schemas.openxmlformats.org/markup-compatibility/2006"
    mc:Ignorable="d">

    <Grid Background="{ThemeResource ApplicationPageBackgroundThemeBrush}">
        <TextBlock x:Name="appTitle" HorizontalAlignment="Center"
        Margin="0,10,0,0" TextWrapping="Wrap" Text="Skype Chat Demo"
        VerticalAlignment="Top"/>
        <TextBox x:Name="skypeName" Margin="0,0,0,100" TextWrapping="Wrap"
        Text="" VerticalAlignment="Center" HorizontalAlignment="Center"
        Width="200" PlaceholderText="Skype ID?"/>
        <AppBarButton x:Name="skypeMessageButton" Click="skypeMessageButton_
        Click" HorizontalAlignment="Stretch" Icon="Message" Label="Send
        Message" Margin="100,0,0,20" VerticalAlignment="Bottom"/>
        <AppBarButton x:Name="skypeCallButton" Click="skypeCallButton_
        Click" HorizontalAlignment="Center" Icon="Phone" Label="Call User"
        Margin="0,0,100,20" VerticalAlignment="Bottom"/>
    </Grid>
</Page>
```

C#

```csharp
using System;
using Windows.System;
using Windows.UI.Xaml;
using Windows.UI.Xaml.Controls;

namespace SkypeChatDemo
    public sealed partial class MainPage : Page
    {
        public MainPage()
        {
            this.InitializeComponent();
        }

        private async void skypeCallButton_Click(object sender,
        RoutedEventArgs e)
        {
```

```
            if(skypeName.Text != "")
            {
                await Launcher.LaunchUriAsync(new Uri("skype:" + skypeName.
                Text + "?call"));
            }
        }

        private async void skypeMessageButton_Click(object sender,
        RoutedEventArgs e)
        {
            if (skypeName.Text != "")
            {
                await Launcher.LaunchUriAsync(new Uri("skype:" + skypeName.
                Text + "?chat"));
            }
        }
    }
}
```

You too can have your own application's protocol so other apps can launch from the launcher. To create a new, unique protocol for your app, you can declare it through the Declarations tab in the appxmanifest file of your solution (Figure 8-6).

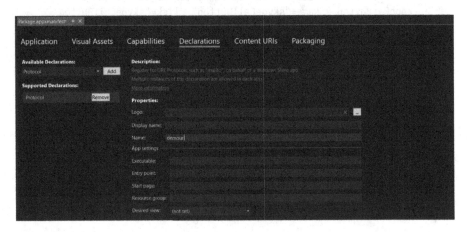

Figure 8-6. *Declaring a protocol in appxmanifest*

App-to-App Communication

How do we communicate? We humans communicate in two ways, through verbal communication and non-verbal communication. Verbal communication includes speaking and listening in a particular language, and non-verbal communication includes sign language, emotional responses, and so on. A girl squeezing an adult's little finger (a.k.a. pinky) tightly is a sign of a heightened emotional response, which could be excited, lonely, or afraid. In other words, it's a signal that both the sender and the receiver understand when passed through any medium sound waves, light waves, or transfer of analog/digital data.

The exchange of data between apps is done in several ways. Some of them are

- Through the clipboard

- Through a shared contract

- Drag and drop

These go in pairs because you need to have a receiver for sender to send something–copy and paste, ShareData, ReceiveData, and drag and drop. Let's take a look at an example (Figures 8-7 through 8-9) where you drag and drop an image anywhere in the app window and copy it to a clipboard operation.

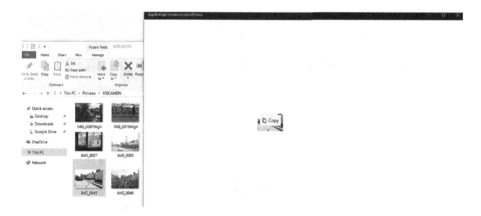

Figure 8-7. *Drag operation being performed*

Figure 8-8. *The image was successfully dropped into the application*

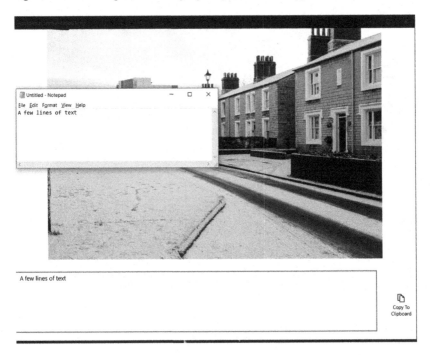

Figure 8-9. *Text was copied to the clipboard and displayed on Notepad*

XAML

```xml
<Page
    x:Class="AppToAppCommunicationDemo.MainPage"
    xmlns="http://schemas.microsoft.com/winfx/2006/xaml/presentation"
    xmlns:x="http://schemas.microsoft.com/winfx/2006/xaml"
    xmlns:local="using:AppToAppCommunicationDemo"
    xmlns:d="http://schemas.microsoft.com/expression/blend/2008"
    xmlns:mc="http://schemas.openxmlformats.org/markup-compatibility/2006"
    mc:Ignorable="d">
    <Grid Background="{ThemeResource ApplicationPageBackgroundThemeBrush}"
    AllowDrop="True" DragOver="sharedImage_DragOver" Drop="sharedImage_Drop">
        <Image x:Name="sharedImage" Margin="0,0,0,200"/>
        <TextBox x:Name="someText" Margin="0,0,100,20" TextWrapping="Wrap"
        Text="" VerticalAlignment="Bottom" Height="150"
        PlaceholderText="write some text here"/>
        <AppBarButton x:Name="clipboardCopy" Click="clipboardCopy_Click"
        HorizontalAlignment="Right" Icon="Copy" Label="Copy To Clipboard"
        Margin="0,0,5,50" VerticalAlignment="Bottom"/>
    </Grid>
</Page>
```

C#

```csharp
using System;
using Windows.ApplicationModel.DataTransfer;
using Windows.Storage;
using Windows.UI.Xaml;
using Windows.UI.Xaml.Controls;
using Windows.UI.Xaml.Media.Imaging;
namespace AppToAppCommunicationDemo
{
    public sealed partial class MainPage : Page
    {
        public MainPage()
        {
            this.InitializeComponent();
        }

        private async void sharedImage_Drop(object sender, DragEventArgs e)
        {
            var img = await e.DataView.GetStorageItemsAsync();
            StorageFile imgFile = img[0] as StorageFile;
            BitmapImage i = new BitmapImage();
            i.SetSource(await imgFile.OpenAsync(FileAccessMode.Read));
            sharedImage.Source = i;
        }
```

```
    private void clipboardCopy_Click(object sender, RoutedEventArgs e)
    {
        if(someText.Text.Length > 1)
        {
            DataPackage dataPackage = new DataPackage();
            dataPackage.RequestedOperation = DataPackageOperation.Copy;
            dataPackage.SetText(someText.Text);
            Clipboard.SetContent(dataPackage);
        }
    }
    private void sharedImage_DragOver(object sender, DragEventArgs e)
    {
        e.AcceptedOperation = DataPackageOperation.Copy;
    }
}
}
```

Asynchronous Operations

You know that a program executes one line at a time. But let's say you are downloading a Visual Studio update synchronously. What will happen is that UI and everything within the application will freeze until the file is completely download to move forward with the next line of the update program. To resolve these situations, asynchronous operations were created. They make the program responsive, so the user doesn't get scared that the program is stuck and requires a reboot.

Asynchronous methods are denoted by the async keyword. This keyword is paired with the await keyword for tasks that need to be done asynchronously. You saw async and await in the previous section where await was used in an event wherever an asynchronous operation took place; it specified that the block of code waited for an event. It is generally used for a task. For this example, you shall perform two tasks to make them wait 1000 and 500 milliseconds, respectively. The output is shown in Figure 8-10.

XAML

```
<Page
    x:Class="AsynchronousOperationDemo.MainPage"
    xmlns="http://schemas.microsoft.com/winfx/2006/xaml/presentation"
    xmlns:x="http://schemas.microsoft.com/winfx/2006/xaml"
    xmlns:local="using:AsynchronousOperationDemo"
    xmlns:d="http://schemas.microsoft.com/expression/blend/2008"
    xmlns:mc="http://schemas.openxmlformats.org/markup-compatibility/2006"
    mc:Ignorable="d">
    <Grid Background="{ThemeResource ApplicationPageBackgroundThemeBrush}">
        <Grid.ColumnDefinitions>
            <ColumnDefinition/>
            <ColumnDefinition/>
        </Grid.ColumnDefinitions>
```

```xml
        <AppBarButton x:Name="task1" Click="task1_Click"
        HorizontalAlignment="Center" Icon="Clock" Label="Task 1"
        Margin="0,0,0,20" VerticalAlignment="Bottom"/>
        <AppBarButton x:Name="task2" Click="task2_Click"
        HorizontalAlignment="Center" Icon="Clock" Label="Task 2"
        Margin="0,0,0,20" VerticalAlignment="Bottom" Grid.Column="1"/>
        <TextBlock x:Name="result1" Margin="10,0" TextWrapping="Wrap"
        Text="" VerticalAlignment="Center" TextAlignment="Center"/>
        <TextBlock x:Name="result2" Margin="10,0" TextWrapping="Wrap"
        Text="" VerticalAlignment="Center" Grid.Column="1"
        TextAlignment="Center"/>
    </Grid>
</Page>
```

C#

```csharp
using System.Threading.Tasks;
using Windows.UI.Xaml;
using Windows.UI.Xaml.Controls;
namespace AsynchronousOperationDemo
{
    public sealed partial class MainPage : Page
    {
        public MainPage()
        {
            this.InitializeComponent();
        }
        private async void task1_Click(object sender, RoutedEventArgs e)
        {
            result1.Text = "";
            result1.Text = await performTask1();
        }
        private async void task2_Click(object sender, RoutedEventArgs e)
        {
            result2.Text = "";
            result2.Text = await performTask2();
        }
        private async Task<string> performTask1()
        {
            await Task.Delay(1000);
            return "Task 1 Completed";
        }
        private async Task<string> performTask2()
        {
            await Task.Delay(500);
            return "Task 2 Completed";
        }
    }
}
```

199

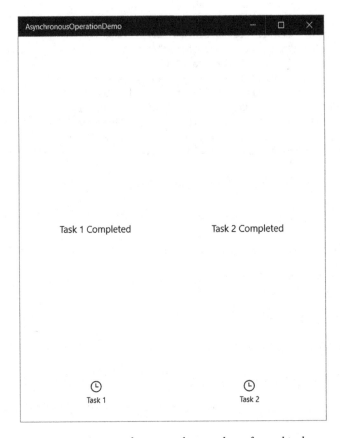

Figure 8-10. *Output of two asynchronously performed tasks*

Multithreading and Parallel Processing

A thread is the smallest unit of programmed instructions managed by a scheduler. Since this book is about simplicity, you are going to experience this concept with another example. In this role, a scheduler is a director that manages budgets, your app is a team leader, and all others (XAML, code behind, resource files, etc.) contribute to employees. When you have purchased your device, a certain amount is donated to the scheduler operating system. This is the hardware specification and it limits the maximum number of resources available to all running programs (including Windows files running in the background). The OS then attempts to make you run your code with the minimum budget possible (single thread). Your app also needs to satisfy the user with a good response time.

Squeezed by this dilemma, your app sometimes needs to request additional employees (threads) to speed up tasks that can run independently. They are identified by the Thread keyword.

Since threads are independent, their resources need to carefully watched. Consider two employees in this example: Sam and Tim. They work in a warehouse of an Internet gifting site. Sam is in charge of packing individual items in boxes and Tim is in charge of providing gift wrapping paper. Sam cannot complete his job without the wrapping paper, and Tim cannot provide the appropriate wrapping paper without knowing the dimensions of the box Sam is using. Tim goes to Sam to ask for the dimensions, but when he reached Sam's office, Sam is busy with some other task, thereby halting Tim in his workflow. In computing terms, this is referred to as a deadlock. These deadlocks can be prevented by meeting the necessary conditions: mutual exclusion, hold and wait, no preemption, and circular wait.

XAML

```
<Page
    x:Class="MultithreadingDemo.MainPage"
    xmlns="http://schemas.microsoft.com/winfx/2006/xaml/presentation"
    xmlns:x="http://schemas.microsoft.com/winfx/2006/xaml"
    xmlns:local="using:MultithreadingDemo"
    xmlns:d="http://schemas.microsoft.com/expression/blend/2008"
    xmlns:mc="http://schemas.openxmlformats.org/markup-compatibility/2006"
    mc:Ignorable="d">
    <Grid Background="{ThemeResource ApplicationPageBackgroundThemeBrush}">
        <Grid.RowDefinitions>
            <RowDefinition/>
            <RowDefinition/>
            <RowDefinition/>
        </Grid.RowDefinitions>
        <TextBox x:Name="totNums" Margin="20,0" TextWrapping="Wrap" Text=""
        VerticalAlignment="Center" PlaceholderText="Numbers to test with"/>
        <AppBarButton x:Name="runButton" Click="runButton_Click"
        HorizontalAlignment="Center" Icon="Clock" Label="Execute" Margin="0"
        Grid.Row="2" VerticalAlignment="Center"/>
        <TextBlock x:Name="forText" HorizontalAlignment="Center"
        Margin="0,0,0,50" Grid.Row="1" TextWrapping="Wrap" Text=""
        VerticalAlignment="Center"/>
        <TextBlock x:Name="parforText" HorizontalAlignment="Center"
        Margin="0,50,0,0" Grid.Row="1" TextWrapping="Wrap" Text=""
        VerticalAlignment="Center"/>
    </Grid>
</Page>
```

C#

```
using System;
using System.Threading.Tasks;
using Windows.UI.Xaml;
using Windows.UI.Xaml.Controls;
```

```
namespace MultithreadingDemo
{
    public sealed partial class MainPage : Page
    {
        public MainPage()
        {
            this.InitializeComponent();
        }
        private static int[] numbers;
        private void runButton_Click(object sender, RoutedEventArgs e)
        {
            int n = Convert.ToInt32(totNums.Text);
            numbers = new int[n];
            Random rand = new Random();
            for (int i = 0; i < n; i++)
            {
                numbers[i] = rand.Next(1, 100); //Generates random integer
                between 1 and 100
            }
            DateTime timer = DateTime.UtcNow;
            for (int i = 0; i < n; i++)
            {
                numbers[i] = 2 * numbers[i] + 3;
                numbers[i] = Convert.ToInt32((numbers[i] - 3) / 2);
            }
            DateTime finished = DateTime.Now;
            TimeSpan timeTaken = finished - timer;

            forText.Text = "For loop took " + timeTaken.Milliseconds + "
            milliseconds.";

            ////Recreates the previous state of numbers array
            numbers = new int[n];
            for (int i = 0; i < n; i++)
            {
                numbers[i] = rand.Next(1, 100); //Generates random integer
                between 1 and 100
            }

            timer = DateTime.UtcNow;
            Parallel.For(0, n, i => {
                numbers[i] = 2 * numbers[i] + 3;
                numbers[i] = Convert.ToInt32((numbers[i] - 3) / 2);
            });
```

```
            finished = DateTime.Now;
            timeTaken = finished - timer;
            parforText.Text = "Parallel for loop took " + timeTaken.
            Milliseconds + " milliseconds.";
        }
    }
}
```

Three test run with different numbers of integers computing the equation $y = 2x + 3$ and reversing to the original by $x = (y - 3)/2$ return the output shown in Figure 8-11.

Figure 8-11. *A parallel for loop versus a for loop in three iterations*

The creation of threads is resource-consuming itself. In this case, a parallel for loop takes more time as the content inside the for loop is basic mathematics and does not require the use of multiple threads. It is advisable to use multithreading and parallel processing if the process inside is a time- and resource-intensive task.

Beyond Physical Contact

You have learned about development using a mouse and keyboard, development with touch inputs, and how to work with images. Now you're going to learn one of the methods to develop stuff that doesn't require input through physical methods. Of course, face detection, facial feature detection, emotion detection are all part of ongoing research and improved algorithms are built continously. But let's explore one of the methods.

You shall target human facial emotion detection because proper implementation of it will be an advantage to your application and will add another dimension to your data: customized feedback based on a user's current emotion state, better targeted advertising, and so on.

There are several approaches to facial emotion detection; you can take inputs from two-dimensional images from geometric methods to a neural network to three-dimensional recognition using Microsoft Kinect. The Viola Jones object detection framework is quite good at facial feature extraction, namely the eyes, nose, and mouth. Once you have extracted the facial features, you may proceed with your own algorithm to detect emotion. Here, I shall discuss one way to do it.

The human mouth consists of the upper lip, a mouth opening, and the lower lip. Here you shall be taking the intensities of the image and its geometric features. After cropping the mouth region, you shall see that by taking the pixel information for every column, there occurs a local minimum (one in case of a closed mouth, and more than one in case of an open mouth) between the upper and lower lip, as demonstrated in Figures 8-12 through 8-15. This occurs on every column even if the right side of the face has been exposed to more light than the left or vice versa.

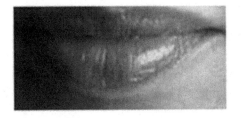

Figure 8-12. *An extracted mouth region*

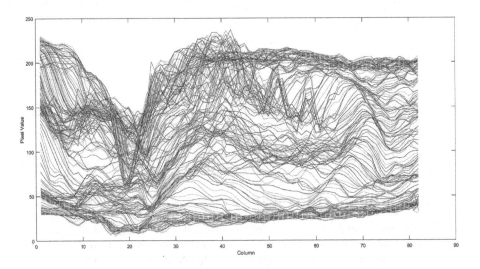

Figure 8-13. *Values of every column*

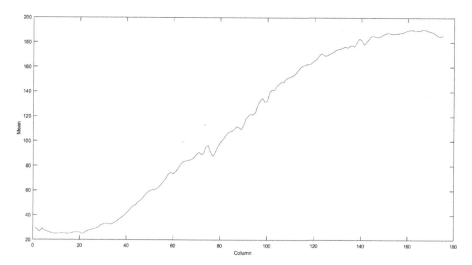

Figure 8-14. *Mean data to see variations in lighting conditions*

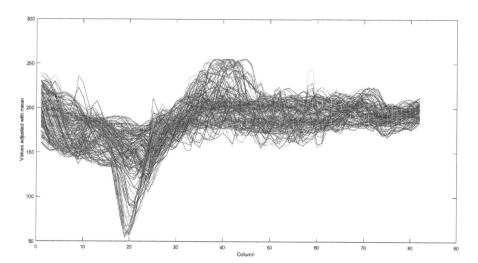

Figure 8-15. *Values of every column with adjusted mean*

In Figure 8-15, you can see the steep dip (minima) around the center of the mouth. Similarly, the detection and implementation of your own algorithm can take your application to another level.

App Intelligence

Previously, I have discussed supervised and unsupervised methods of machine learning in short. Let's explore this deeper in this section. You will build an application that needs to know a user better over time.

Let's build an intelligent application for teens that gives a mathematics problem every day, a "problem of the day" kind of thing. The app needs to understand an individual teen's math level. To do this, it needs some data to judge. The program contains the following parts: rnd is a random number between the upper and lower limit; ans is the expected result; firstNumber and secondNumber are two text boxes that store the first and second number, respectively; symbol is a text block; and pageTitle is another text block that shows the question number.

Addition

```
private void addition()
{
    num1 = rnd.Next(llimit,ulimit);
    num2 = rnd.Next(llimit,ulimit);
    ans = num1 + num2;
    firstNumber.Text = num1.ToString();
    secondNumber.Text = num2.ToString();
    symbol1.Text = "+";
    pageTitle.Text = "Question " + (progressRecord.Value + 1).ToString();
}
```

Subtraction

```
private void subtraction()
{
    num1 = rnd.Next(llimit,ulimit);
    num2 = rnd.Next(llimit,ulimit);
    ans = num1 - num2;
    firstNumber.Text = num1.ToString();
    secondNumber.Text = num2.ToString();
    symbol1.Text = "-";
    pageTitle.Text = "Question " + (progressRecord.Value + 1).ToString();
}
```

Multiplication

```
private void multiplication()
{
    num1 = rnd.Next(llimit,ulimit);
    num2 = rnd.Next(llimit,ulimit);
    ans = num1 * num2;
```

```
    firstNumber.Text = num1.ToString();
    secondNumber.Text = num2.ToString();
    symbol1.Text = "X";
    pageTitle.Text = "Question " + (progressRecord.Value + 1).ToString();
}
```

Division

```
private void division()
{
    num1 = rnd.Next(llimit,ulimit);
    num2 = rnd.Next(llimit,ulimit);
    ans = num1 / num2;
    firstNumber.Text = num1.ToString();
    secondNumber.Text = num2.ToString();
    symbol1.Text = "/";
    pageTitle.Text = "Question " + (progressRecord.Value + 1).ToString() +
    ": Answer upto 2 decimal places";
}
```

Percentage

```
private void percentage()
{
    num1 = rnd.Next(llimit,ulimit);
    if (lastNo == 1 || lastNo == 2)
    {
        num2 = rnd.Next(1,5) * 20;
    }
    else if (lastNo == 2)
    {
        num2 = rnd.Next(1, 9) * 10;
    }
    else
    {
        num2 = rnd.Next(1, 99);
    }
    ans = num1 * num2 / 100;
    firstNumber.Text = num2.ToString() + "%";
    secondNumber.Text = num1.ToString();
    symbol1.Text = "of";
    pageTitle.Text = "Question " + (progressRecord.Value + 1).ToString() +
    ": Answer upto 2 decimal places";
}
```

Estimation

```
private void estimation()
{
    num1 = rnd.Next(llimit,ulimit);
    num2 = rnd.Next(1,llimit) * 10;
    firstNumber.Text = num1.ToString();
    secondNumber.Text = num2.ToString() + "s";
    symbol1.Text = "to the nearest";
    double nhigh = Convert.ToInt32(Math.Ceiling((double)num1 / num2)*num2);
    double nlow = Convert.ToInt32((double)Math.Floor(num1 / num2)*num2);
    ans = (nhigh - num1) <= (num1 - nlow) ? nhigh : nlow;
    pageTitle.Text = "Question " + (progressRecord.Value + 1).ToString();
}
```

Discounting

```
private void discounting()
{
    num1 = rnd.Next(llimit,ulimit);
    if (lastNo == 1 || lastNo == 2)
    {
        num2 = rnd.Next(1, 5) * 20;
    }
    else if (lastNo == 2)
    {
        num2 = rnd.Next(1, 9) * 10;
    }
    else
    {
        num2 = rnd.Next(1, 99);
    }
    firstNumber.Text = num2.ToString() + "%";
    secondNumber.Text = num1.ToString();
    symbol1.Text = "off";
    ans = num1 - (num1 * num2 / 100);
    pageTitle.Text = "Question " + (progressRecord.Value + 1).ToString() +
    ": Answer upto 2 decimal places";
}
```

Note that rnd is of the Random class, num1 is a randomly generated number, and num2 is the second randomly generated number between the lower and upper limits (called llimit and ulimit, respectively). The result can be checked by matching the user inputted result with the correct result. These are some of the possibilities to make your application better. The variable for each mathematical section is the range of values a user is comfortable with. For instance, someone may face difficulty multiplying three-digit numbers while another person may find it easy. So, for the first couple of days the app tries to vary the range of inputs and collects the users' performance data. Once that is done, your algorithm must segment the data into two categories, satisfactory (80% success rate or higher) and unsatisfactory, to establish a clear boundary. The specific algorithm you use in your application is purely your own application's design. You may choose to start from day 1 with an unsupervised approach or throw in random limits and proceed with a supervised approach once you have an ample amount of data to train your app.

A very simple unsupervised clustering algorithm is k-means. K-means clustering aims to maximize the distance between two cluster means while minimizing the distance between each sampled data and a single cluster mean with each iteration. For execution of a standard k-means, we generally consider Euclidian distance and k clusters, giving the number of cluster means.

The execution of the algorithm starts by sampling k data units from the whole population (whole data). These are marked as mean (μ) of the cluster. All the other data are then mapped into k clusters by computing their distance from the means as minimize (μ – Data). This is the first iteration of the algorithm. For the second iteration, the means of the clustered classes are taken as an input mean for the iteration. The algorithm then continues for a predefined N number of iterations.

To illustrate this with an example, let's take a look at an examination grading system. Student performance in Table 8-1 shows the actual marks earned by 10 students on a scale of 100. If they were to be linearly scaled such that the maximum mark achieved by the group gets scaled up to 100 and then is divided into grades A, B, and C such that A is greater than or equal to 75, B is between 40 and 75, and C is below 40, then 5 students get a grade of A. But with k-means clustering, only 2 students get a grade of A with centroids at 77, 61.75, and 22.5 of the original student performance scores. So, when a new student comes with a performance mark of 75, the student falls under

Minimum of (77-75, 75-61.75, 75-22.5)

= Minimum of (2, 13.25, 52.5) or the centroid 77 is the closest, meaning the student gets a grade A.

Table 8-1. *Comparison of Two Marking Models, Linearly Scaled and K-Means Clustering, with Centroids at 77, 61.75, and 22.5*

Student Performance	Grade	
	Scaled	K-Means
16	20 – C	C
79	100 – A	A
31	39 – C	C
53	67 – B	B
17	22 - C	C
60	76 - A	B
26	33 - C	C
65	82 - A	B
69	87 - A	B
75	95 - A	A

This is all well and good. But one day the class decides to skip the examination, so they all end up with the same score (0, as shown in Table 8-2). On a linearly scaled marking model, all the students wind up with a 100. And on a k-means clustering model, all the students wind up receiving more than one grade, which we know is not feasible. Even if a new student comes and scores a 20, the new student will still end up with all three grades as minimum of (20-0, 20-0, 20-0) are the same. The marking model can therefore, in this situation, flag the examination with k-means clustering.

Table 8-2. *Comparison of Two Marking Models, Linearly Scaled and K-Means Clustering, with Centroids at 0, 0, and 0*

Student Performance	Grade	
	Scaled	K-Means
0	100 – A	A, B, C
0	100 – A	A, B, C
0	100 – A	A, B, C
0	100 – A	A, B, C
0	100 – A	A, B, C
0	100 – A	A, B, C
0	100 – A	A, B, C
0	100 – A	A, B, C
0	100 – A	A, B, C
0	100 – A	A, B, C

Machine learning (supervised, unsupervised, or semi-supervised) is used today to make applications more intelligent. Semi-supervised is where only a part of the population to be used for training is labelled. A use that you may recognize is in fitness bands. Such algorithm constantly collects and trains your data to determine and cluster the distance and height differences between walking, running, climbing stairs, and other activities.

EXERCISES

Exercise 1: Build an inking application for a mobile device and a traditional laptop/desktop without touch. How would you optimize your controls for a touch screen and on a laptop where the user is drawing using a trackpad?

Exercise 2: Using an asynchronous task, fetch images from Bing's image search.

Exercise 3: Build two applications, a sender and a receiver, to transfer an image file.

Exercise 4: Implement a protocol for your application.

Exercise 5: Once you have grasped the concepts well, take a sound file of people conversing in a language you do not understand as input, and cluster it into different sound waves in spatial and frequency domains to see if you can extract phrases of a language.

CHAPTER 9

███

Cross Platform with Xamarin

People say that the sky's the limit. You are going to touch the sky! You are no longer burdened by the questions of where you should begin or where the market is trending. No matter which mobile operating system is dominating the market, your app has reached it already.

Xamarin is owned by Microsoft (as I am authoring this book) and is headquartered in California, USA. Xamarin is the name of the company and also their product (a cross-platform development platform). Of course, as company names go, Xamarin also has a company type attached to it such as Xamarin Inc., Xamarin Ltd., and so on depending on the laws of the countries where branches of the company are located and the type of work (main objectives of the company) the country branch handles.

Construction professionals build buildings, but it is the responsibility of an architect to design a masterpiece. When working with cross-platform development (or even simple UWP for that matter), I strongly recommend that you not fuss about which programing language to use or start building right away. What you are *doing* takes precedence over *how* you are going to implement it. Brainstorming sessions between you and your team prior to designing the architecture are very important.

Cross-platform development places several new challenges on your application's architecture. One such example is the way people/users/consumers have adapted to an operating system's experience. In my opinion, Macintosh users are used to a single mouse button click rather than three (left, right, scroll wheel) on Windows. Linux users are comparatively more relaxed using a command-line interface than Windows or Macintosh users.

Think about your mouse and keyboard. For a right-handed person, the mouse is placed on the right side of the keyboard. The experience for a left-handed person is shown in Figure 9-1.

© Ayan Chatterjee 2017
A. Chatterjee, *Building Apps for the Universal Windows Platform*,
DOI 10.1007/978-1-4842-2629-2_9

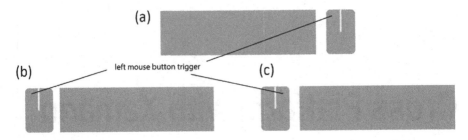

Figure 9-1. Mouse control for a right-handed user (a) and possible mouse controls for a left-handed user (b and c)

You can imagine the hurdles for a left-handed user to overcome if the left and right mouse clicks are suddenly switched towards and far away from the keyboard. These are some of the aspects to keep in mind when developing cross-platform applications. Your application must be built to fit into someone's life naturally.

Xamarin Architecture

With Xamarin, your application's architecture is divided into shared elements and platform-specific elements (Figure 9-2). The shared elements are the business logic, data layers, service access layers; all of the compatible NuGet packages that you may have used in UWP remain. The platform-specific elements are the UI elements, application layer, metadata, and things specific to a platform.

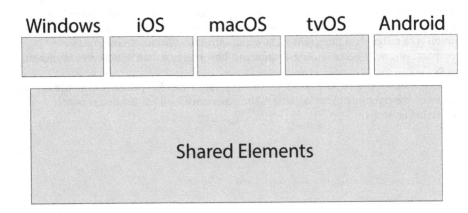

Figure 9-2. Cross-platform development application architecture

Installing in Visual Studio

Installing Xamarin in Visual Studio is a straightforward process. All you need to do during your Visual Studio installation is select the Xamarin checkbox and everything will be installed for you. Figure 9-3 shows the installation options in Visual Studio 2017. Apart from Xamarin in Visual Studio, you also have an option to install it for your PC or your Mac as a standalone from Xamarin's website.

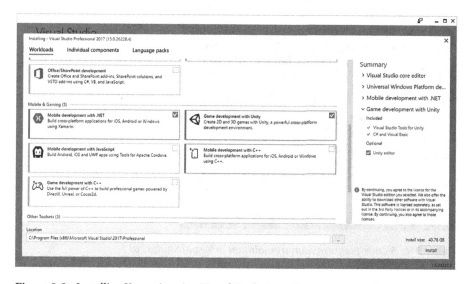

Figure 9-3. *Installing Xamarin using Visual Studio Installer*

If you recall, I covered the Windows 8 family of solutions where one universal solution was divided into several individual projects (phone, desktop, etc.) and they had a shared code project. Take a look at Figure 9-4; if you have grasped the previously discussed topics, then you are already aware of how cross-platform development works with Xamarin, apart from slight changes in development, deployment, and release. There are individual projects for iOS, Android, and UWP with one project for shared code.

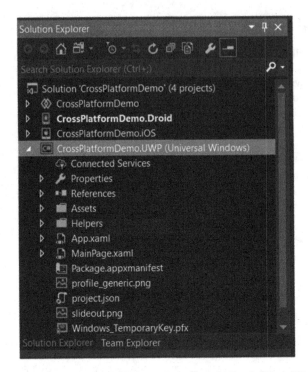

Figure 9-4. A cross-platform Xamarin solution in Visual Studio 2017

Xamarin for iOS and macOS

macOS and iOS are Apple's desktop and mobile operating systems, respectively. Before going into details with Xamarin, let's first explore how applications are built in Apple's native development environment, Xcode. Swift and Objective-C are the programming languages used in Xcode (Swift is relatively new). You will first dive into iOS app development using Apple's native Xcode and then move to Xamarin to compare how similar they are.

Xcode is a development IDE (integrated development environment) for Apple's family of operating systems. To install Xcode on your Mac, all you need to do is go into the Mac App Store and install Xcode like any regular app and everything's automatically done for you. Figure 9-5 shows the home page of Xcode where you can see the following three options presented to you on the left-hand side:

- The Playground is where you get to code and see the output in real time as you are programing. It is best used to quickly implement and test a piece of code without actually going through the process of creating a new project.

- You can create a new Xcode project from scratch using project templates for various platforms.

- You can open an existing project from a repository.

Figure 9-5. *Xcode home page on macOS*

For your purposes, you will create a new project because you wish to be familiar with the iOS app development process in order to quickly grasp the concepts used in cross-platform development with Xamarin. When you click the **Create a new Xcode project** option, the screen shown in Figure 9-6 opens up with various project templates for iOS, watchOS, tvOS, macOS, or cross-platform (if you wish to build an app for both iOS and macOS platforms in one project).

Figure 9-6. *Xcode project templates for iOS*

You are now presented with some project templates, single view application being the simplest one because it's a single page. Some of the others are master-detail (like the Settings app), page-based (like the iOS home page itself), and tabbed application (like a click app with tabs for world clock, alarm, bedtime, stopwatch, and timer). You can start off with a single view application and add more views (pages) and arrange them as master-detail, tabbed, or any other, and even make them nested or add your own transition effects.

Let's create a new single view application, as shown in Figure 9-7. You may wonder about Core Data. You can use Core Data to locally store data as you would do with a database, and you can use standard Objective-C or Swift code to perform operations like fetch requests. By now, unit tests and UI tests should be familiar to you. To learn more about Core Data and how to use it in your applications, detailed documentation can be found on the Apple Developer website (`https://developer.apple.com/reference/coredata`).

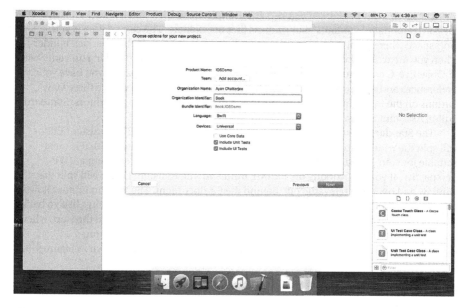

Figure 9-7. *Creating a new iOS project*

If you recall the components of the solution covered in previous chapters, the project settings shown in Figure 9-8 should look familiar to you. They consist of identity information, signing information for developer identification, minimum target version, supported orientations, device capabilities, and so on.

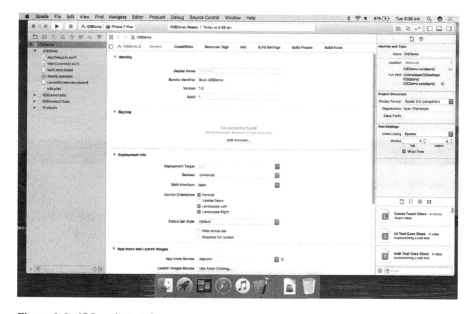

Figure 9-8. *iOS project settings*

Let's take a deeper look at Figure 9-8 and explore the UI. The left side (known as the Navigator pane) contains your projects files and folders. The central area is your workspace where whatever you are focusing on opens up, such as the interface builder when you are working on your storyboard, the editor when you are working on your Swift or Objective-C code, and so on. To the right (known as the Utility pane), you have your preferences and asset catalog. You can show or hide these sections via the three view buttons on the top right. And beside the view buttons to the left are the editors: Standard Editor, Assistant Editor, and Version Editor.

The Standard Editor is the default and is what you are seeing. The Assistant Editor will split the window into two and simultaneously show you the window that is most suitable for your primary work document. To understand this concept from a UWP perspective, if you are working on a XAML front end, the Assistant Editor will split the window and open the relevant code behind the C# document. The Version Editor allows you to switch and review different versions of your file and you can do things like go back to an earlier version of a swift file, view changes you have made right from the start, when and who made changes to your code if connected to a repository, and so on.

Moving on with the development process, let's assess assets, as shown in Figure 9-9.

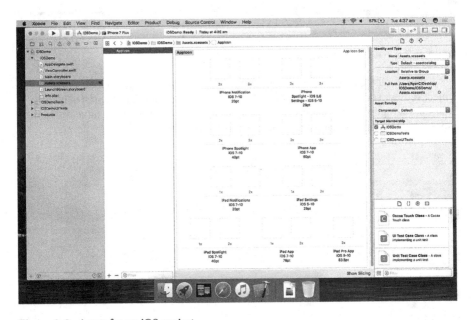

Figure 9-9. *Assets for an iOS project*

Similar to UWP, iOS apps support scalable assets. The syntax compared to UWP is shown in the following examples:

Example 1: 100% (original size)

```
UWP: filename.scale-100.fileextension
iOS: filename@1x.fileextension
```

Example 2: 200% (scaled up)

```
UWP: filename.scale-200.fileextenstion
iOS: filename@2x.fileextenstion
```

To summarize, the iOS scalable asset syntax is

```
filename@scale.fileextenstion
```

Plist or property list (Figure 9-10) is similar to the manifest file for UWP applications. It specifies application details, device family, OS version details, the application's desired orientations, launch image, capabilities, and so on. It is a key-value pair list containing keys that are specific to the types of systems: iOS, macOS, watchOS, cocoa, core foundation, and app extensions like a notification widget.

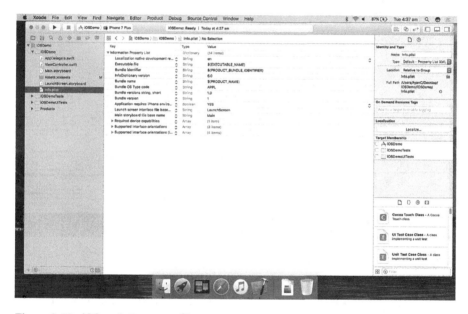

Figure 9-10. *iOS project property list*

This raises a very crucial point. If you are new to this and have come across content from other sources that cover keyboard shortcuts to all kinds of menus, just ignore that. Learning is a process and such shortcuts should come naturally after you are familiar with the UI components. It's just like moving to a new city. At first, you use a maps application and try to stay on major roads. Once you get used the city, you learn to take shortcuts through alleys and narrow paths to get to your destination faster.

Now that you have set up a project, it is time to dive in and start building it. The **Storyboard** (completely different from Storyboard Animations in UWP) is where you build your views (pages), page elements, and page flows, and where you define behaviors such as page transitions using **Interface Builder** in Xcode.

221

Unlike Windows or Android, iOS devices are limited to a subset of Apple devices, which means as a developer you know the devices and the hardware capabilities you are dealing with–no more, no less. Figure 9-11 shows the layout controls of a UI element. This narrows down your UI design into only a few choices, such as

- Portrait layout for iPhone

- Landscape for small and standard iPhone

- Landscape for iPhone Plus devices

- iPad

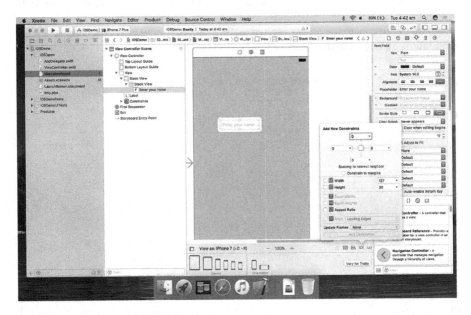

Figure 9-11. *Layout controls in Xcode*

There are two types of UI elements: those that let you do something like press a button and those where the code behind does something and you get the output on a display. Action and Outlet will be discussed when we move to Xamarin but for the time being, imagine two parties at play here: you and the code behind content. The UI element does something only when either you or the code behind pokes it (sends some instructions). The direction the instructions come from makes an element either an Action or an Outlet.

```
User -> UI Element <- Code Behind
```

Figure 9-12 shows that a textbox can be both Action or Outlet or can contain an Outlet Collection. Once you have defined an element as an Action or Outlet or both, events are created for it by dragging and dropping the event connector to your code behind and a window pops up to define your event (shown in Figure 9-13) and to assign a property name to a UI element (Figure 9-14).

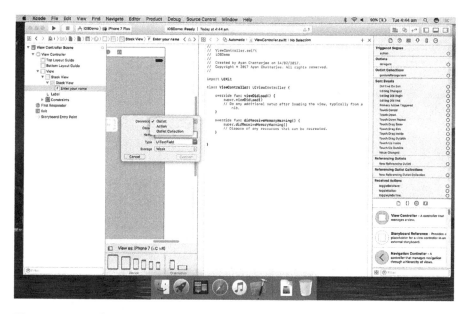

Figure 9-12. *UI element types*

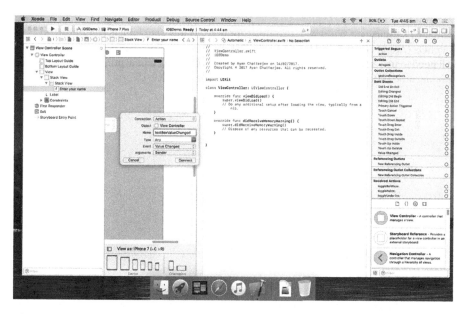

Figure 9-13. *Creating an iOS event*

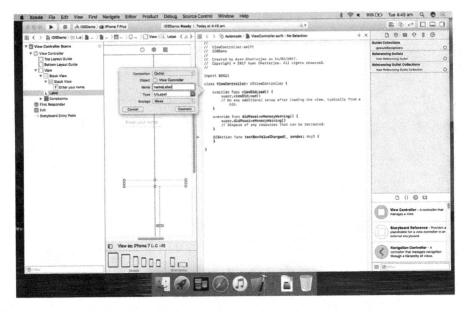

Figure 9-14. *Assigning a property name to an UI element*

You have just briefly explored iOS application development. Let's get back to Xamarin. Xamarin on Windows currently support development for iOS (iPhone, iPad), watchOS (Apple Watch), and tvOS (Apple TV) applications. For macOS development, you will need to use Xamarin on a Macintosh computer. Creating a new project is as simple as creating an UWP project in Visual Studio, as shown in Figure 9-15.

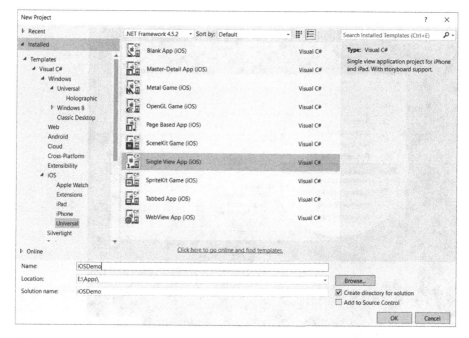

Figure 9-15. *Creating a new iOS single view application in Visual Studio*

However, to use Xamarin for iOS app development inside Visual Studio, you need to connect it to a Mac due to policy, legal, business model, and other restrictions and agreements that Xamarin has with Apple. Figures 9-16 and 9-17 show how to connect a Mac with Xamarin Mac Agent, thus allowing Interface Builder to be accessed (Figure 9-18). The rest of the process is straightforward and you shall build simple Xamarin iOS application that changes background color with RGB sliders.

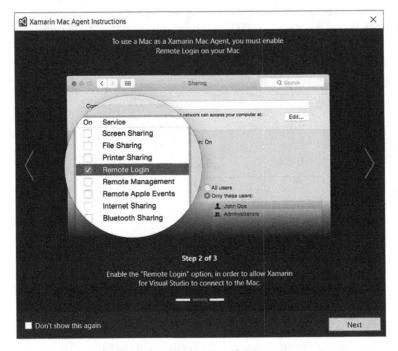

Figure 9-16. Remote access to a Mac is required for several capabilities in Xamarin for iOS

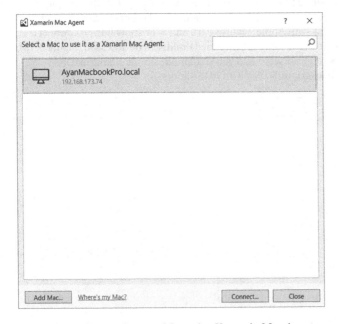

Figure 9-17. Connecting to a Mac using Xamarin Mac Agent

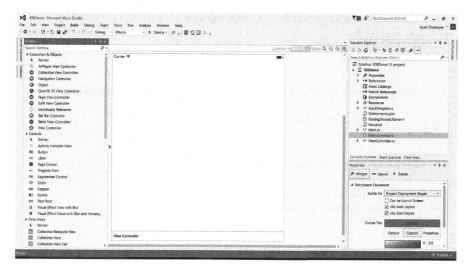

Figure 9-18. *Xamarin iOS Designer in Visual Studio*

C#

```csharp
using System;
using UIKit;

namespace iOSDemo
{
    public partial class ViewController : UIViewController
    {
        byte r = 127, g = 127, b = 127;
        public ViewController(IntPtr handle) : base(handle)
        {
        }

        public override void ViewDidLoad()
        {
            base.ViewDidLoad();
            updateViewColor();
            RedSlider.ValueChanged += RedSlider_ValueChanged;
            BlueSlider.ValueChanged += BlueSlider_ValueChanged;
            GreenSlider.ValueChanged += GreenSlider_ValueChanged;
        }
```

```
private void GreenSlider_ValueChanged(object sender, EventArgs e)
{
    g = Convert.ToByte(GreenSlider.Value);
}

private void BlueSlider_ValueChanged(object sender, EventArgs e)
{
    b = Convert.ToByte(BlueSlider.Value);
}

private void RedSlider_ValueChanged(object sender, EventArgs e)
{
    r = Convert.ToByte(RedSlider.Value);
    updateViewColor();
}

private void updateViewColor()
{
    ColorChangeView.BackgroundColor = new UIColor(red: r / 255,
    green: g / 255, blue: b / 255, alpha: 1);
}

public override void DidReceiveMemoryWarning()
{
    base.DidReceiveMemoryWarning();
    // Release any cached data, images, etc that aren't in use.
}
}
}
```

Now let's dive into Xamarin for macOS on a Macintosh machine to show how similar they are, no matter what OS you are building on. You'll use Xamarin.Mac to bring your Visual Studio applications to the millions of Mac users all over the world. When you click on a new project, you get four options to create a mac app: Cocoa, SpriteKit Game, SceneKit Game, and the most recent, Metal Game. Metal was released about the same time the Swift programing language was released to the public. You will move forward with Cocoa as an example (Figure 9-19).

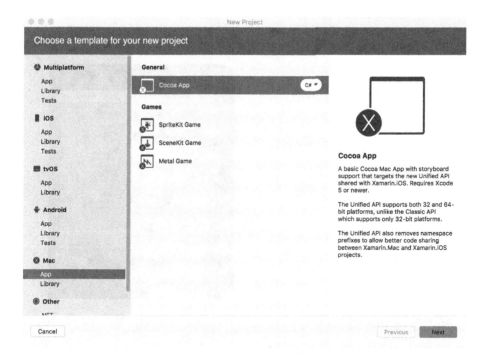

Figure 9-19. *New project as Cocoa app*

The Cocoa application uses the model-view-controller (MVC) architecture. Model is your business logic/code behind, view is the front-end user interface, and controller is what links the front-end elements with the code behind.

In Figure 9-20, you enter in the app's basic information such as name, organization identifier (meant to be the reverse of your web URL, so if your company URL is samplename.com, the identifier should be com.samplename), extensions (a document-based application like a PDF reader application that can open multiple documents at the same time, each in its own window), and minimum macOS target. Figure 9-21 shows the additional options required for a Cocoa application like where the project is stored, version control, etc. Figure 9-22 shows the Interface Builder for a Cocoa application.

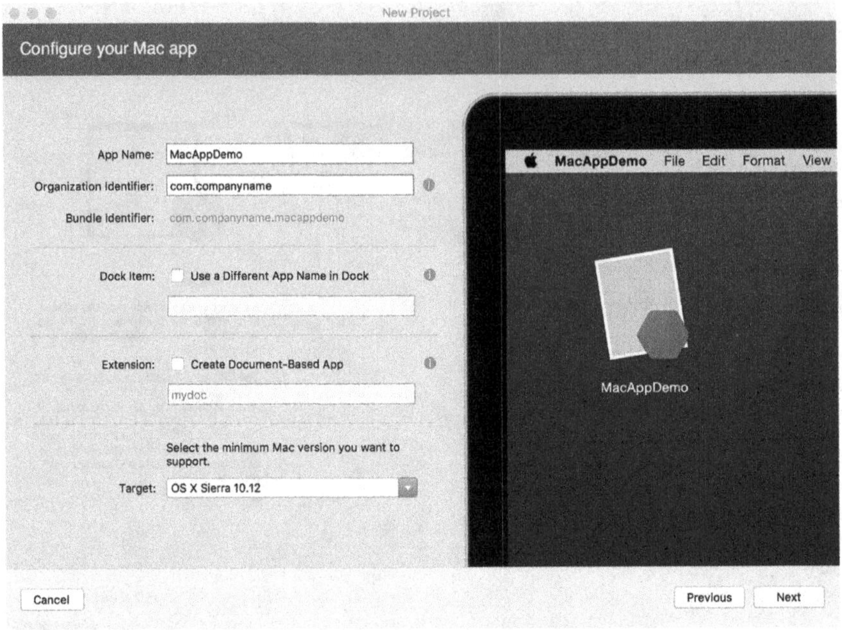

Figure 9-20. *Introductory information for the Cocoa application*

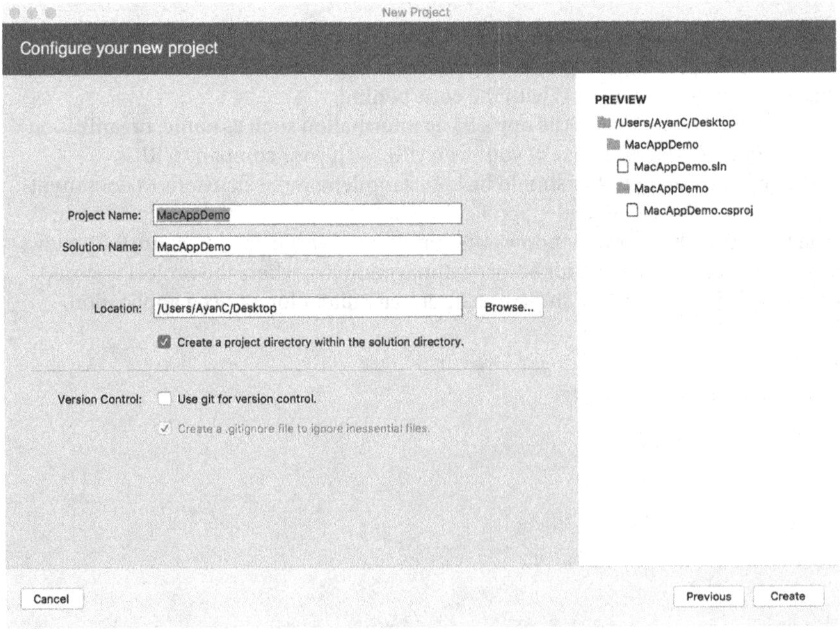

Figure 9-21. *Additional options for the app created in Figure 9-20*

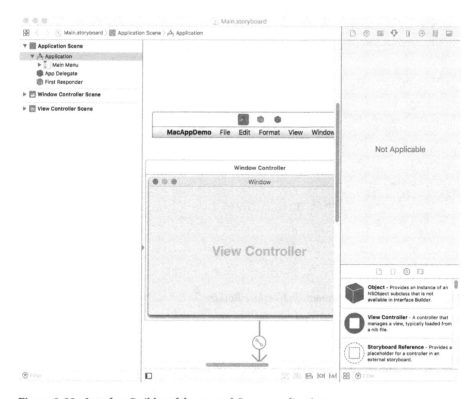

Figure 9-22. *Interface Builder of the created Cocoa application*

While building your application, you may across the two file extensions of Interface Builder: **xib** and **nib**. Note that nib is short for NeXT Interface Builder, and xib is short for XML Interface Builder and is more recent file structure of Interface Builder. As a developer, you need not worry about them. You should focus on your objective only. A writer shouldn't care if the work is being stored in doc, docx, pages, or any other format as long as that work is stored somewhere and the writer is able to work with any application of his/her choice. Getting back to the development process, similar to Figure 9-14 where you declared elements of an iOS application, Figure 9-23 shows how to assign elements of a Cocoa application.

```
// WARNING
// This file has been generated automatically by Xamarin Studio to
// mirror C# types. Changes in this file made by drag-connecting
// from the UI designer will be synchronized back to C#, but
// more complex manual changes may not transfer correctly.


#import <Foundation/Foundation.h>
#import <AppKit/AppKit.h>


@interface ViewController : NSViewController {
    NSTextField *randomNumberButton;
}

- (IBAction)clickMeButton:(id)sender;
@property (assign) IBOutlet NSTextField *randomNumberButton;

@end
```

Figure 9-23. *Declaring elements in Interface Builder*

Next, you need to jump to the ViewController header file and add your outlets (IBOutlet) and actions (IBAction) for the user interface elements, as shown in Figure 9-23.

Action: View (front end) ➤ View Controller (code behind)

Outlet: View Controller (code behind) ➤ View (front end)

You can think of it this way: action in Apple development refers to anything that is provoked when a user does something like click a button or a touch event on an object, whereas outlet is something that updates a UI element through your code. For this example, the button is an action and the label is an outlet. So when the user clicks the button, the code will generate a random number and output it in the label.

When you are done with the UI (xib file) in Xcode, you will go back to Xamarin to continue writing the code behind. Xamarin will automatically create View Controller and View Controller Designer with the UI elements for you to dive into the code. The rest of the process is the regular C# syntax as defined in Xamarin.Mac. Figure 9-24 shows the output of this demo application.

Figure 9-24. *Output of macOS demo application*

View Controller Designer

```
using Foundation;
using System.CodeDom.Compiler;

namespace MacAppDemo
{
        [Register ("ViewController")]
        partial class ViewController
        {
                [Outlet]
                AppKit.NSTextField randomNumberButton { get; set; }

                [Action ("clickMeButton:")]
                partial void clickMeButton (Foundation.NSObject sender);

                void ReleaseDesignerOutlets ()
                {
                        if (randomNumberButton != null) {
                                randomNumberButton.Dispose ();
                                randomNumberButton = null;
                        }
                }
        }
}
```

View Controller (C#)

```csharp
using System;
using AppKit;
using Foundation;

namespace MacAppDemo
{
        public partial class ViewController : NSViewController
        {
                public ViewController(IntPtr handle) : base(handle)
                {
                }

                public override void ViewDidLoad()
                {
                        base.ViewDidLoad();

                        // Do any additional setup after loading the view.
                }

                public override NSObject RepresentedObject
                {
                        get
                        {
                                return base.RepresentedObject;
                        }
                        set
                        {
                                base.RepresentedObject = value;
                                // Update the view, if already loaded.
                        }
                }

                partial void clickMeButton(NSObject sender)
                {
                        Random rand = new Random();
                        randomNumberButton.StringValue = "Number = " + rand.
                        Next(1, 1000).ToString();
                }
        }
}
```

Xamarin for Android

Visual Studio is to Windows what Xcode is to Mac. Similarly, Android Studio is Google's native IDE for Android application development (Figures 9-25 and 9-26).

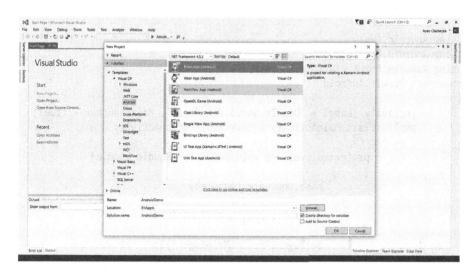

Figure 9-25. *Creating a new Xamarin.Android application*

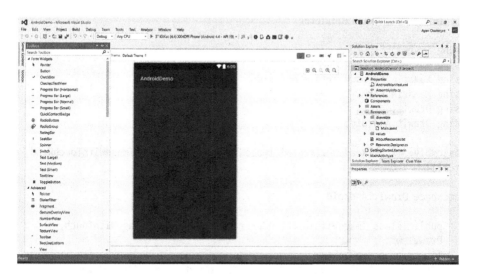

Figure 9-26. *Blank page of a newly created Xamarin.Android application*

I covered iOS and macOS application development in Xamarin in detail; Android is no different other than what is in the front end. I assume you are now familiar with application development in Xamarin. For the Android app demo, let's create something a bit more complex: a paint canvas. The code below is a hint and I'll let you fill in the blanks.

Main Activity

```
using Android.App;
using Android.OS;
using Xamarin.Forms.Platform.Android;
namespace DrawIt.Android
{
        [Activity (Label = "DrawIt.Android.Android", MainLauncher = true)]
        public class MainActivity : FormsApplicationActivity
        {
                protected override void OnCreate (Bundle bundle)
                {
                        base.OnCreate (bundle);

                        Xamarin.Forms.Forms.Init (this, bundle);

                        SetPage (App.GetMainPage ());
                }
        }
}
```

Image with Touch Renderer

```
using System;
using System.ComponentModel;
using Xamarin.Forms.Platform.Android;
using Xamarin.Forms;
using DrawIt;
using DrawIt.Android;

[assembly: ExportRenderer(typeof(ImageWithTouch), typeof(ImageWithTouchRenderer))]

namespace DrawIt.Android
{
    public class ImageWithTouchRenderer : ViewRenderer<ImageWithTouch,
    DrawView>
    {
        protected override void OnElementChanged(ElementChangedEventArgs
        <ImageWithTouch> e)
        {
            base.OnElementChanged(e);
```

```
        if (e.OldElement == null)
        {
            SetNativeControl(new DrawView(Context));
        }
    }

    protected override void OnElementPropertyChanged(object sender,
    PropertyChangedEventArgs e)
    {
        base.OnElementPropertyChanged(sender, e);

        if (e.PropertyName == ImageWithTouch.CurrentLineColorProperty.
        PropertyName)
        {
            UpdateControl();
        }
    }

    private void UpdateControl()
    {
        Control.CurrentLineColor = Element.CurrentLineColor.ToAndroid();
    }
    }
}
```

Apart from using specific UWP, iOS, macOS, or Android templates, you could build for all of them together using Xamarin Forms Application using XAML and C#. There is currently a gap to fill. The gap is that Xamarin forms do not have a graphical designer; hopefully they will build one in a future iteration. For now, if you are comfortable with and confident enough to write XAML and C# right away, please move ahead with Xamarin Forms.

Deployment and Store-Ready

Submitting apps to the iOS or Mac App Store requires an Apple Developer subscription. Figure 9-27 shows the home page of Apple developer website (developer.apple.com). Similar to the growth of Windows Store and Windows Phone store into one UWP Windows Store, previously subscriptions for iOS and Mac developer programs were separate, but recently all of iOS, Mac, watchOS, and tvOS have merged into one Apple Developer Program.

Figure 9-27. *Apple Developer website*

With developer.apple.com you manage your own or your enterprise subscription, authorized personnel on your team and their individual roles, create documentation, and so on but your applications are managed through iTunes Connect (itunesconnect. apple.com). You can think of iTunes Connect similar to Windows Dev Center where you reserve app names, manage metadata, upload store icons and screenshots, manage your app's pricing, and receive analytics data as and when users start downloading and using your application.

In Figures 9-28 through 9-35, you can see the publication process inside iOS, macOS, and Android to get you familiar with them.

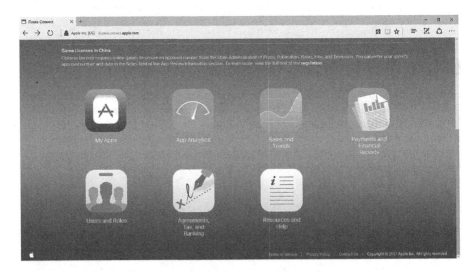

Figure 9-28. *iTunes Connect home page*

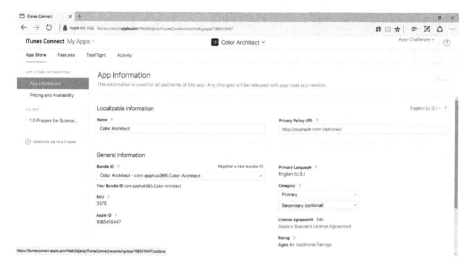

Figure 9-29. *iOS application information metadata on iTunes Connect*

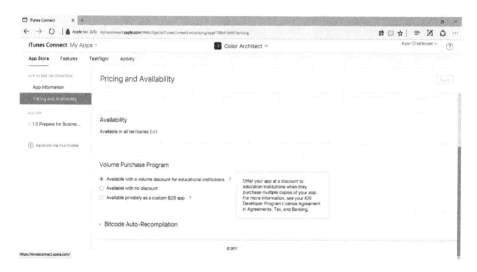

Figure 9-30. *iOS application pricing and availability*

Figure 9-31. IAP for iOS application on iTunes Connect

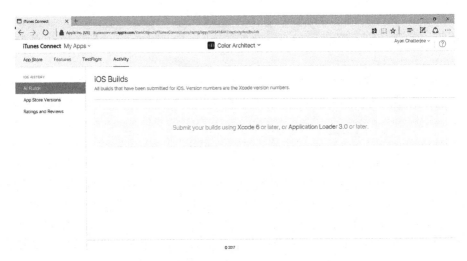

Figure 9-32. iOS application build submission

Figure 9-33. *iOS application analytics*

For Android, there is a Google Play Developer website (developer.android.com) and Console, as shown in Figure 9-34. The remaining process is the same, from uploading a built package to putting it live in the store (Figure 9-35).

Figure 9-34. *Android Developer website*

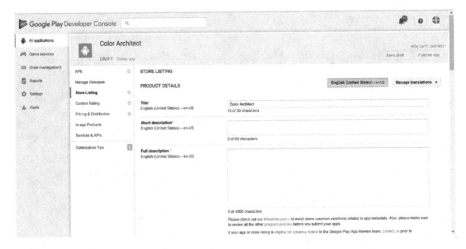

Figure 9-35. *Android application metadata*

After reading this chapter, a thought may come across your mind. The deployment procedure for UWP, iOS, macOS, Android, and others are similar. All of them require you to have a login, upload built applications, put in some metadata, go through testing procedures, and get published in their respective stores. Then how are they different? It boils down to the models that each company prefers for their products and their day-to-day operating procedures, be it business model, distribution model, or licensing model. An obvious conclusion is that Apple's model is more controlled end-to-end whereas Microsoft and Google have a more generous model for other companies to build their own innovative products for the worldwide market.

EXERCISES

Exercise 1: Build sample programs that employ multithreading in both Xamarin.iOS and Xamarin.Android.

Exercise 2: Build a mac application to capture a photo from a webcam (facetime camera) and save it to your local disk.

Exercise 3: Experiment with biometric authentication and build a sample program for both iOS and Android devices.

Exercise 4: Being familiar with the design and development process of cross-platform applications, if you were in charge of designing a UI designer for Xamarin Forms, how would that go? Brainstorm on it.

CHAPTER 10

■ ■ ■

Ready for the Store

You have come all the way through the development process but this is where I request
that you take a beat and try to be cautious. If you or your company is in the early stages or
a start-up stage, I'd like to draw your attention to something that can keep you away from
potential danger. Let's say you or your team has invented an improved bicycle wheel.
But you cannot put it in a bicycle and sell it in the market right away. This is because
even though you own the wheel, you do not own the rest of the parts of the bicycle. This
does not mean that you cannot sell them all together, but it does mean that you need
the appropriate permissions from the owners of the rest of the parts. This stage is where
partnerships, negotiations, and memorandums take place.

Intellectual property is a very important concept. It protects your rights as well as
the rights of others. The organizations who handle this will be able to provide specific
information applicable to your state/country. In my view, they are three kinds of
intellectual property:

- **Stuff you can use without permission:** This stuff might come
  with additional constraints such as whatever you reuse cannot be
  used for profit or you need to acknowledge the original owner(s).

- **Stuff you need some kind of permission to use:** This is mainly
  corporate-owned property or inventions that have been patented.
  The owned body will provide specific instructions on how to
  obtain the permission.

- **Stuff that are not available for reuse/release/classified:** This stuff
  belongs to some body of the government and may be exclusive
  to that particular part of the government. This category may also
  include a new idea that a researcher is working on or a new concept
  that a company is experimenting within the company itself.

■ **Tip** It is important to be informed of the intellectual property laws applicable to your region.

This chapter deals with the essentials steps required for a UWP application to be
prepared and submitted to the Windows Store for public download. If you have followed
through every chapter in this book and if you are prepared to submit your app to the
Store, let's take a look at how.

© Ayan Chatterjee 2017
A. Chatterjee, *Building Apps for the Universal Windows Platform*,
DOI 10.1007/978-1-4842-2629-2_10

Assets

I covered scalable assets in a previous chapter. For UWP, you need to define different resolutions of tiles, logos, and icons in the Visual Assets section of appxmanifest, as shown in Figure 10-1.

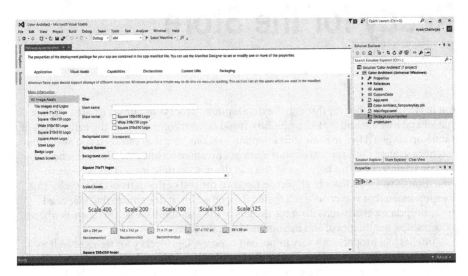

Figure 10-1. *Visual assets in the Application Package Manifest*

Visual Studio displays the images that you need. Figure 10-2 shows the sizes of scale-based assets.

Scale-based assets

Category	Element name	At 100% scale	At 125% scale	At 150% scale	At 200% scale	At 400% scale
Small	Square71x71Logo	71x71	89x89	107x107	142x142	284x284
Medium	Square150x150Logo	150x150	188x188	225x225	300x300	600x600
Wide	Square310x150Logo	310x150	388x188	465x225	620x300	1240x600
Large (desktop only)	Square310x310Logo	310x310	388x388	465x465	620x620	1240x1240
App list (icon)	Square44x44Logo	44x44	55x55	66x66	88x88	176x176

Figure 10-2. *Scale-based assets as shown in Windows Dev Center documentation*

Manifest

Application package manifest (appxmanifest) is an XML document (don't worry; there's a good GUI in Visual Studio) that contains information for the system to deploy your app seamlessly. In UWP, there are six tabs for the package manifest.

- **Application**

    The name of your application, entry point of your application, default language to use in your application, description, whether or not your application requires lock screen notifications, and live tile updates if you are updating the tile remotely (see Figure 10-3).

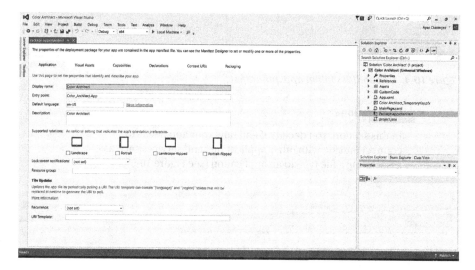

Figure 10-3. Application tab in appxpmanifest

- **Visual assets**

    I covered this in the previous section.

- **Capabilities**

    If you require any capabilities in your application to make it run smoothly, not enabled by default, such as user account information, webcam, microphone, phone call, contacts, and others, set them here (see Figure 10-4).

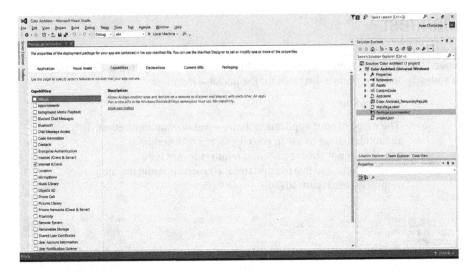

Figure 10-4. *Capabilities tab in appxpmanifest*

- **Declarations**

  In this section, you declare if and how your app needs to connect outside with other applications and services such as associating a file type to an application (see Figure 10-5).

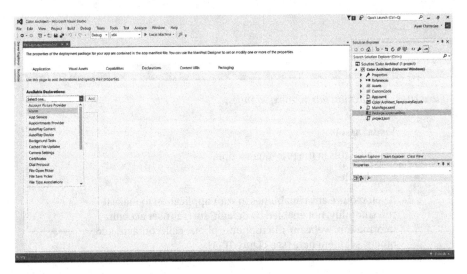

Figure 10-5. *Declarations tab in appxpmanifest*

- **Content URIs**

  Enables you to create a link to external websites
  (see Figure 10-6).

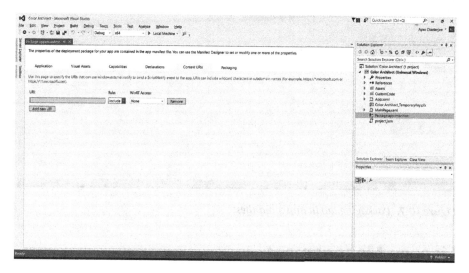

Figure 10-6. *Content URI tab in appxpmanifest*

- **Packaging**

  Contains the unique identity of your application on
  Windows Store with information such as package name,
  version information, publisher identification, and so on
  (see Figure 10-7).

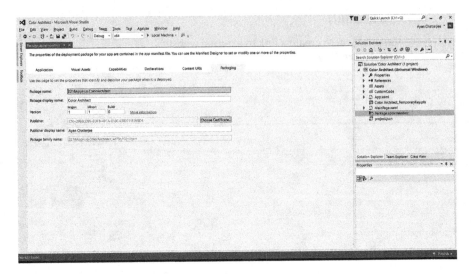

Figure 10-7. Packaging tab in appxpmanifest

License Management

License and certificate management forms an integral part of the software deployment process. It verifies the integrity and security of the software and the identity of the organization from which it came. For a Macintosh application, the following steps are taken before an application is deployed from Mac App Store:

- Read-only privileges of the data layer

- Codesign of third party (registered developer/organization)

- Codesign of Apple from Apple Worldwide Relations Certifications Authority

In UWP, an application's identity is shown in Figure 10-8. Specific details have been struck off from the image.

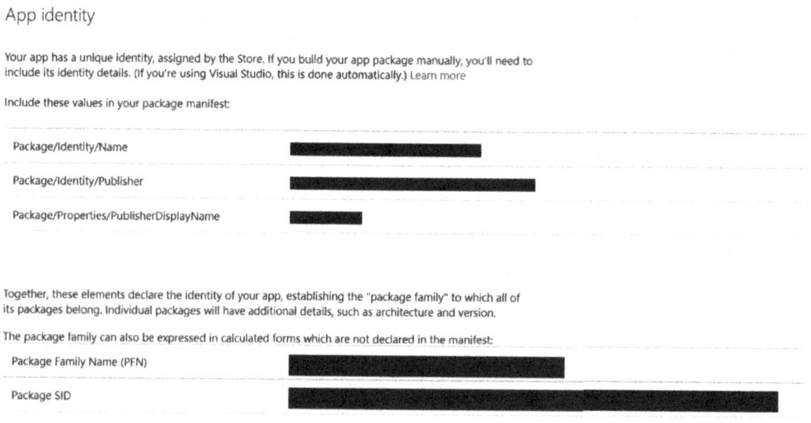

App identity

Your app has a unique identity, assigned by the Store. If you build your app package manually, you'll need to include its identity details. (If you're using Visual Studio, this is done automatically.) Learn more

Include these values in your package manifest:

Package/Identity/Name ███████████████████

Package/Identity/Publisher █████████████████████████

Package/Properties/PublisherDisplayName ████████

Together, these elements declare the identity of your app, establishing the "package family" to which all of its packages belong. Individual packages will have additional details, such as architecture and version.

The package family can also be expressed in calculated forms which are not declared in the manifest:

Package Family Name (PFN) ██████████████████

Package SID █████████████████████

Figure 10-8. *An application's identity*

Windows Store Settings

Before submitting an application to the store, the appropriate application identity of the app must match with that of a reserved application name in Windows Store. You can view your application's details in the manifest file and also when you edit the project file (by unloading the project and editing, as shown in Figure 10-9).

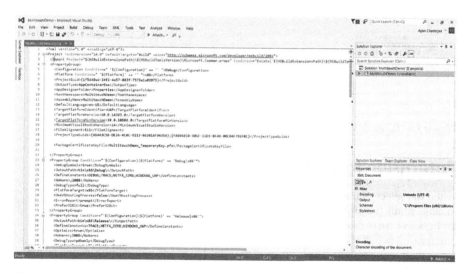

Figure 10-9. *Editing a project*

If you are not sure about what you are doing, Visual Studio does it for you. Simply right-click your project, go to **Store**, and click the **Associate App with the Store** option, as shown in Figure 10-10. Visual Studio automatically sets it up for you.

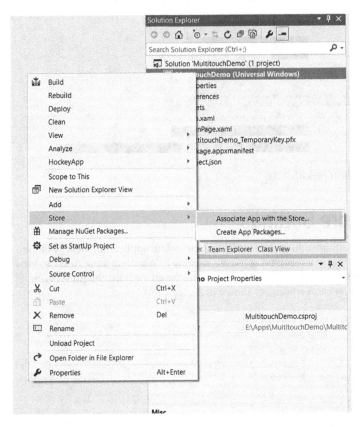

Figure 10-10. *Associating your app with Windows Store*

Enterprise Ready

When you select your application to be distributed to Windows Store for businesses to make a bulk (volume) purchase, your app gets published to the Windows Store for Business. An organizational purchaser (a person who has the authority to make a purchase on behalf of an organization) can then purchase your application in volume as per their requirements. The licenses of the application will naturally be owned by the organization. The person with this authority can assign licenses to people within the organization and even reclaim them as necessary.

When the organization pays for licenses upfront, the employees browsing and viewing the applications get them for free. Organizations can also include/disable access to applications from the public store and only display applications assigned to the organization's private store. In summary, an organization's private store may display the following:

- Applications from the public store (Windows Store)

- Applications purchased by the organization assigned to the private store

- An organization's internal line-of-business (LOB) applications

To make your application available to the Windows Store for Business, all you need to do is enable it in the organizational licensing section when you publish your application, as shown in Figure 10-11.

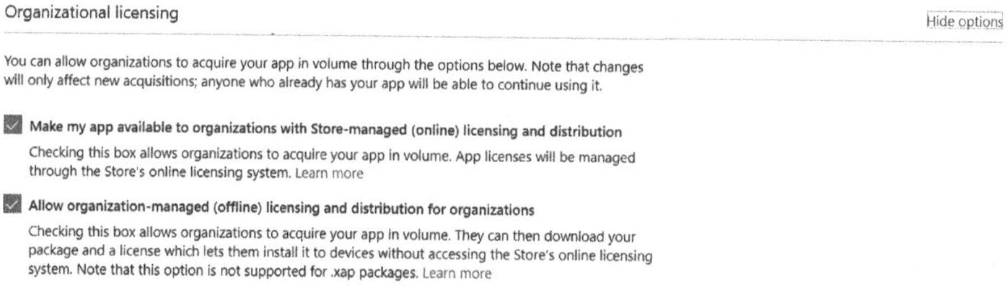

Organizational licensing   Hide options

You can allow organizations to acquire your app in volume through the options below. Note that changes will only affect new acquisitions; anyone who already has your app will be able to continue using it.

☑ Make my app available to organizations with Store-managed (online) licensing and distribution
   Checking this box allows organizations to acquire your app in volume. App licenses will be managed through the Store's online licensing system. Learn more

☑ Allow organization-managed (offline) licensing and distribution for organizations
   Checking this box allows organizations to acquire your app in volume. They can then download your package and a license which lets them install it to devices without accessing the Store's online licensing system. Note that this option is not supported for .xap packages. Learn more

Figure 10-11. Organizational licensing in Windows Dev Center

For LOB apps, an organization who wants your product must invite you first. Once they invite you and you accept that invitation, you can then publish for LOB distribution. The rest of the process remains the same for the developer.

Store Submission and Evaluation

Now that you are prepared for your application to be public, it is time to submit it to the Windows Store for certification and publication. The first step is to reserve a unique name for your application. You must be sure that your application's name meets all the necessary requirements, one of which is that it does not violate someone else's trademark. After that, there are five things to take care of before your app moves forward:

- Pricing and availability

- Properties

- Age ratings

- Packages

- Store listings

- Notes for certification (optional)

Under pricing and availability (Figure 10-12), you specify the price of your application (free/paid/paid with trial); the number of markets your app should be available in; sale pricing, if you wish to put it on sale for a certain period of time; distribution, where you control if the app is public, LOB, or other; the organizational license model it uses (as shown in Figure 10-11); and publication date (if you wish to publish on a particular date or set it to publish as soon as your app passes certification).

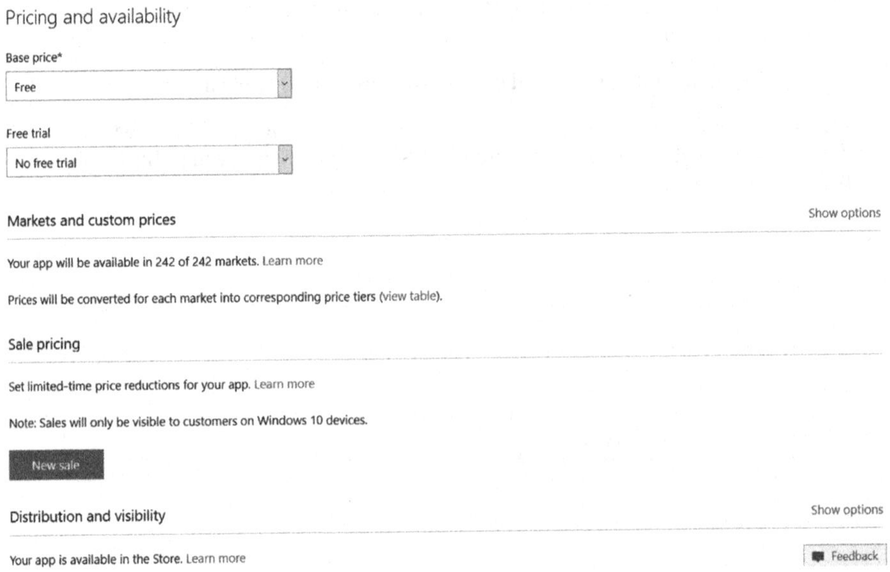

Figure 10-12. *Pricing and availability for Windows Store submission*

Properties (Figure 10-13) is where you define under which category your app best fits, product declarations where you declare certain factors about your app such as accessibility guidelines, and system requirements where you define the minimum and recommended hardware requirements a user must have to run your application properly.

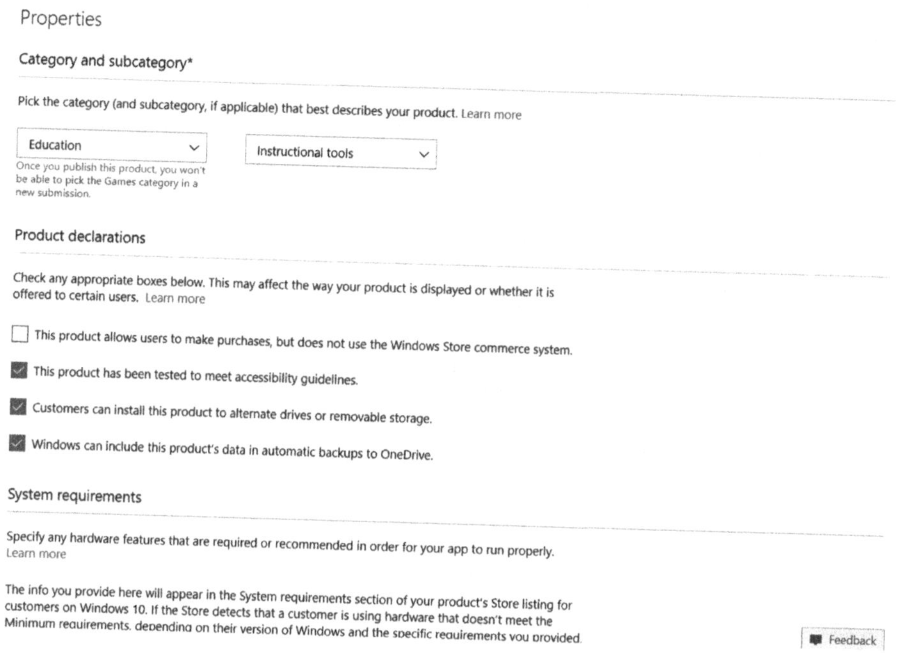

Properties

Category and subcategory*

Pick the category (and subcategory, if applicable) that best describes your product. Learn more

| Education ∨ | Instructional tools ∨ |

Once you publish this product, you won't
be able to pick the Games category in a
new submission.

Product declarations

Check any appropriate boxes below. This may affect the way your product is displayed or whether it is
offered to certain users. Learn more

☐ This product allows users to make purchases, but does not use the Windows Store commerce system.

☑ This product has been tested to meet accessibility guidelines.

☑ Customers can install this product to alternate drives or removable storage.

☑ Windows can include this product's data in automatic backups to OneDrive.

System requirements

Specify any hardware features that are required or recommended in order for your app to run properly.
Learn more

The info you provide here will appear in the System requirements section of your product's Store listing for
customers on Windows 10. If the Store detects that a customer is using hardware that doesn't meet the
Minimum requirements, depending on their version of Windows and the specific requirements you provided.

💬 Feedback

Figure 10-13. *Properties for Windows Store submission*

With age ratings (Figure 10-14), you are able to convey to the audience if they are of
appropriate age to use the application.

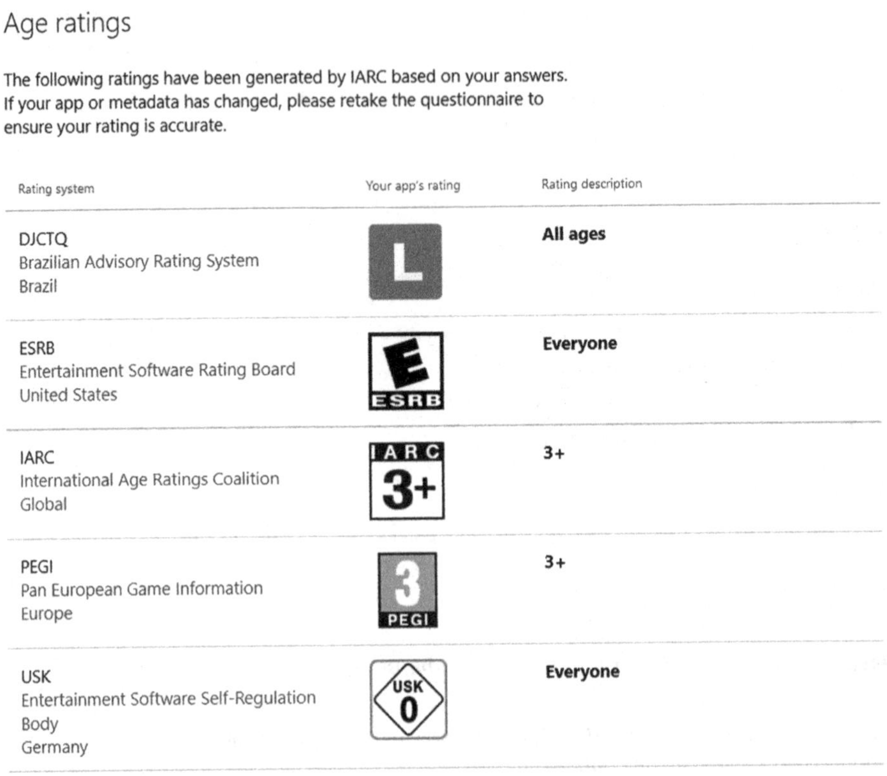

Age ratings

The following ratings have been generated by IARC based on your answers. If your app or metadata has changed, please retake the questionnaire to ensure your rating is accurate.

Rating system	Your app's rating	Rating description
DJCTQ Brazilian Advisory Rating System Brazil	L	**All ages**
ESRB Entertainment Software Rating Board United States	E ESRB	**Everyone**
IARC International Age Ratings Coalition Global	IARC 3+	**3+**
PEGI Pan European Game Information Europe	3 PEGI	**3+**
USK Entertainment Software Self-Regulation Body Germany	USK 0	**Everyone**

Figure 10-14. *Age ratings for Windows Store submission*

Packages (Figure 10-15) is where you upload your app packages to the Windows Store and specify if they are for Windows 10 Desktop, Windows 10 Mobile, Windows 10 XBOX, Windows 10 Holographic, and/or made for previous versions of Windows.

Packages

If you are using Visual Studio, be sure you signed in with the same account associated with your developer account, as some parts of the package are specific to this account. Learn more

Drag your packages here (.xap, .appx, .appxbundle, .appxupload) or browse your files.

Device family availability

This table shows which packages will be offered to specific Windows 10 device families (and earlier OS versions, if applicable) in ranked order. If a device family's box is unchecked, new customers on that type of device won't be able to acquire the app (though customers who already have the app can still use it, and will get any updates you submit). Learn more

☑ Let Microsoft decide whether to make this app available to any future device families

Packages	Windows 10 Desktop	Windows 10 Mobile	Windows 10 Xbox	Windows 10 Holographic	Windows 8/8.1	Windows Phone 8.x and earlier
	☑	☑	☐	☐		

Figure 10-15. *Packages for Windows Store submission*

Store Listings is where you input your application's metadata such as description, release notes, screenshots, support, and other information. This is information that people see while browsing Windows Store. The Notes for Certification section is optional; it's where you share privately to people certifying your application notes about your app. These notes may be the username and password for a test account of your application, steps to access hidden features in your application, and so on.

Once you are done, your app will pass through the Windows Store certification process and will get published if everything is okay.

Windows 10 Deployment vs. Previous Versions

This section is not really relevant to your development process but I thought to include it for the knowledge and so you can see how deployment has progressed. Prior to Windows Store's deployment model, individual companies used to license and distribute their application on their own. Enterprise software companies would even get software delivered via email from their contractors. Games and applications used to be distributed by CDs, DVDs, and other physical media. With Windows Store in the Windows 8 family, the Windows 8 desktop store and mobile stores were separate from each other. As it grew, Windows Store managed to come together in one distribution platform. All of this is not a change in what you or a company builds, it is just a systematic way to do it.

CHAPTER 11

Application Analytics

This is a good time to look at the software development life cycle (SDLC). SDLC is a standard procedure for how apps should be built, starting from the first step (having an idea) to the last (entering the market). There are many SDLC models, like Agile and waterfall, but all flow from brainstorming and planning sessions to testing and implementation. Let's take a look at the cycle.

1. **Initiation**

   It all begins when you have a new, original idea.

2. **Software Concept Development**

   This is when you brainstorm on the original idea and how to make it feasible.

3. **Planning**

   You need a good project management workflow with stakeholders, deliverables, and milestones.

4. **Requirement Analysis**

   Now that you know what you are going to build, you need to decide what hardware/software to work with, and whether to work with UWP, Xamarin, or something else.

5. **Design**

   Here, you build your application's design and workflow with UML diagrams.

6. **Development**

   You build the first prototype of your application in Visual Studio.

7. **Test**

   You run some quality assurance tests with unit tests, performance tests, and even human testers.

© Ayan Chatterjee 2017
A. Chatterjee, *Building Apps for the Universal Windows Platform*,
DOI 10.1007/978-1-4842-2629-2_11

8. **Implementation**

    Your application's first version goes live on Windows Store for
    the world to use.

9. **Maintenance**

    You perform some bug fixes and performance enhancements
    on the current version.

10. **Disposition**

    Unless you are shutting down your application and taking it
    off the Store, you realize that your current version needs to
    be replaced by a new one. You may add new features to the
    current version or do a complete refresh, in which case you go
    back to step 1.

All of the previous chapters talked about design, development, testing, and
implementation where you build your application and publish it in Windows Store or any
other store. In this chapter, I will be taking about step 9, maintenance.

Getting insight into your application's day-to-day performance and acting upon it
to provide continuous support and updates is what keeps your application flourishing
in the market. You should test your application with performance measurement tools
in Visual Studio before submission. But there are things to do after you start getting
user's data. Windows Dev Center documentation has laid out some of their performance
measurement responsiveness suggestions with respect to time. Table 11-1 and Figure 11-1
summarize the information.

Table 11-1. *Summary (column 2 and 3 representing the respective minimum
and maximum) of User Responsiveness Performance Suggestion*

Fast	100 milliseconds	200 milliseconds
Typical	300 milliseconds	500 milliseconds
Responsive	500 milliseconds	1 second
Launch	1 second	3 seconds
Continuous	500 milliseconds	5 second
Captive	500 milliseconds	10 second

Figure 11-1. *Summary of Table 11-1*

Windows Store Analytics

The Windows Store developer portal provides detailed analytics of your published application. Despite all of your unit tests and other tests, when your application performs in the real world, there will be bugs. Windows Store Analytics is a good place to test your application's performance. Apart from that, you also get to know the demographics of the users who have downloaded your application. Let's explore Windows Store Analytics.

The **Acquisitions** screen tells you how many new users have downloaded your application by market (Figures 11-2, 11-3, and 11-4). You can filter by market (country) and the version of Windows, and by demographic (Figure 11-5) with age groups and gender.

Acquisitions

Market

| All markets | ∨ |

OS version

| All OS versions | ∨ |

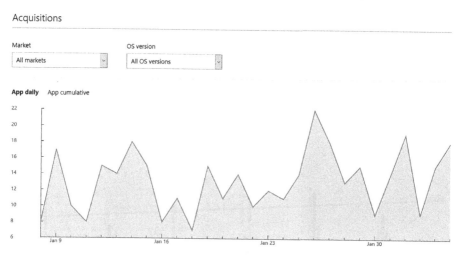

Figure 11-2. *Windows Store app acquisitions*

Markets

Market	Acquisitions ∨
United States	146
India	44
United Kingdom	37
Mexico	14
Canada	12
France	9
Germany	8
Indonesia	8
Brazil	7
Spain	7

OS version

Windows 10	207
Windows 8.1	107
Windows Phone 8.1	58
Windows Phone 7.5	8
Windows 8	4
Windows Phone 8	3

Download ↓

Figure 11-3. *Acquisitions by market and OS version*

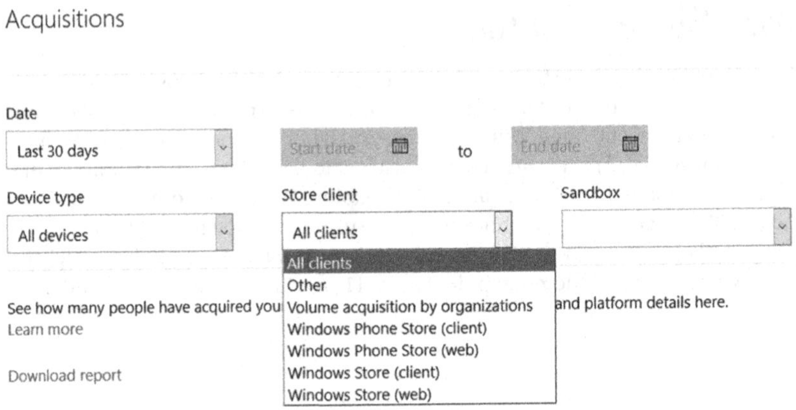

Acquisitions

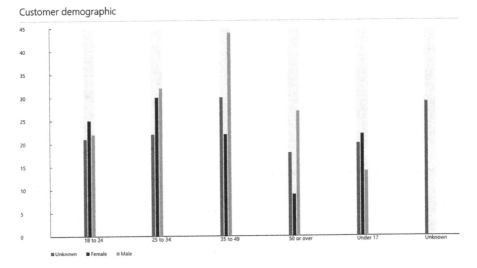

Figure 11-4. *Windows Store Analytics filters*

Customer demographic

Figure 11-5. *Customer demographic*

If you have an in-app purchase model in your application, it will show up in the **add-on acquisitions** section. **Installs** will show you how many users have recently installed your application. **Usage** (Figure 11-6) will show you how many users are actively using your application as well as the not so active ones.

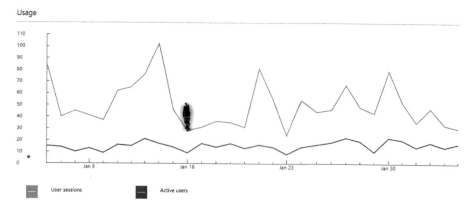

Figure 11-6. *User sessions and active users*

Health will display how your application is performing out there in the world. It gives you information about the number of times the application has crashed (Figure 11-7) including the market (country) where it occurred, the datetime, the device it occurred on (Figure 11-8), and the function requiring attention.

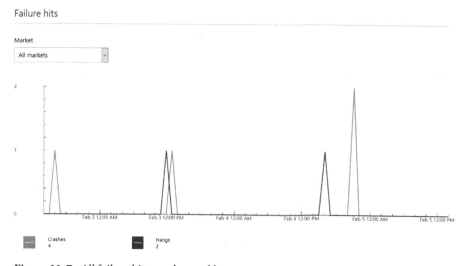

Figure 11-7. *All failure hits–crashes and hangs*

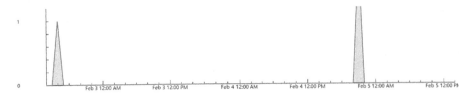

Download ⬇

Failure log

Date ⌄	Package version	Device type	Device model	OS build	Links
02/04/2017 9:29:29 PM	2.1.0.0	Unknown	LENOVO-20266	6.3.9600	Stack trace
01/26/2017 11:33:44 AM	2.1.0.0	Unknown	Intel Corporation-Intel powered classmate PC	6.3.9600	Stack trace
01/26/2017 11:11:10 AM	2.1.0.0	Unknown	Intel Corporation-Intel powered classmate PC	6.3.9600	Stack trace
01/26/2017 10:27:35 AM	2.1.0.0	Unknown	Intel Corporation-Intel powered classmate PC	6.3.9600	Stack trace
01/23/2017 9:50:59 AM	2.1.0.0	Unknown	Unknown	6.3.9600	Stack trace
01/16/2017 5:12:08 PM	2.1.0.0	Unknown	TOSHIBA-SATELLITE L10W-B-101	6.3.9600	Stack trace

Figure 11-8. Failure log

Ratings and **Reviews** display your application's user ratings and user feedback, including feedback from Windows insiders. **Channels and conversions** show from where the users (who are downloading) are coming to your application. It also lets you measure your campaign's performance. There are other details such as advertising performance if you have enabled in-app advertising.

Visual Studio Mobile Center

Azure is Microsoft's suite of cloud solutions. It ranges from just hosting a website to detailed analytics, and collection and processing large amounts of data (big data) including Cortana Intelligence Suite. It is not restricted to UWP and Windows Solutions but pretty much anything you can think of. So apart from basic Windows Store Analytics, if you wish to collect more custom data or perform some machine intelligence, you do it through Azure.

In the early days, usage and crash analytics were collected on a module in the Azure portal. This was during the Windows 8/8.1 era. Later on, the functionality was migrated to **HockeyApp**. Presently, it is being migrated to Visual Studio Mobile Center (`https://mobile.azure.com`), shown in Figure 11-9. (When I say *being migrated*, it means at the time of writing this book).

Figure 11-9. Visual Studio Mobile Center home page

With each iteration of analytics solutions, the functionalities keep upgrading. For example, with HockeyApp you can distribute, manage crashes, and perform analytics on your iOS, Android, and UWP applications. And with Xamarin Test Cloud you can run tests on thousands of devices available in the market without owning a mobile device yourself.

Visual Studio Mobile Center is the next generation and it contains all of the previous features combined into one bundle, including signing and distribution of your app builds to your app testers in one place. For a single application, be it UWP, iOS, or Android, there are the following options:

- **Build** is where you upload your coded application like the ipa file for an iOS application.

- **Test** is where you test on several physical devices such as iPhone 6 running iOS 9, iPhone 6 running iOS 10, iPhone 7 running iOS 10.1, and so on, based on your filters and the devices you wish to test on.

- **Distribute** is where you send successful test builds to test groups.

- **Groups** is where you assign different testers to tester groups for your application.

- **Releases**, **Tables**, **Identity**, **Crashes**, and **Analytics**

All of the things you can do in the UI in Mobile Center can be done through command line using APIs (https://docs.microsoft.com/en-us/mobile-center/).

Actionable Data

It would feel a bit incomplete without talking a bit about statistics. Although we didn't go deep with deep learning but I feel I've given you the foundation and intuition for you to grow towards it. But once you have built a classifier, how are you going to evaluate it? We know that autonomous cars use computer vision and machine learning to identify potential vehicles in front of the car. Actually, it uses deep learning (deep is when a machine learning algorithm has a lot of hidden layers) and artificial neural network to get the job done but we are not going into too much details on that in this book. Such newly developed algorithm is first tested on known situations. For the purposes of explanation, let's say that we have 10,000 images labelled (meaning all the objects in those images are marked). And we use 10% or 1,000 images for training a machine learning model and the rest for cross-validation. From cross-validation, we know how many vehicles are accurately detected by the algorithm and how many are not. This forms 4 categories of results - true positive, false positive, true negative, false negative. Think of it as 'condition' and 'known'. For true, or in other words for the condition part, predicted result matches with the known result. So, true positive would be vehicles that are really vehicles and the algorithm was able to successfully classify them as vehicles. Similarly, false positive would be vehicles that are really vehicles but the algorithm could not classify them correctly. And if you want to know answers to questions like how many objects were incorrectly marked as vehicles? The result would be in the number of false negatives. Statistical computations like confusion matrix, F1 score, kappa statistic, etcetera all rely on these 4 categories for every class. Six sigma is one of the statistical techniques to improve performance and quality. For performance improvement measurement efforts, DPMO (defects per million opportunities) is measured. You may implement whichever one you prefer, but Six Sigma is one of the industry standards. It was originally designed for manufacturing industries. Table 11-2 shows the DPMO against sigma level.

Table 11-2. *DPMO and Percentage Defective Against Sigma Level*

Sigma Level	DPMO	Percentage Defective
1	691462	69%
2	308358	31%
3	66807	6.7%
4	6210	0.62%
5	233	0.023%
6	3.4	0.00034%
7	0.019	0. 0000019%

You can interpret it this way: when your application performs at 5 sigma level, about 233 users are experiencing hangs and crashes among a million users. An application works perfectly if it is performing at 6 sigma level. Taking action on this analytical data is very essential. It tells you what you can do to make your application perform better and increase your reach.

If a fault is occurring on a specific device, you can use device-specific code. If a country is performing very well and another poorly for your application, you can redirect your advertising model to target that poorly performing market and grow your sales. If one bug is affecting 10,000 users and another is affecting 200 users, the one affecting more users gets precedence. This is how you should handle bug fixes and maintenance updates: systematically.

To conclude this chapter and this book, I'd like to thank you. Whether you are in high school, or in college trying to capture the next big idea with your friends in a dorm room, whatever it is that you do or are trying to do, the approach to solving a complicated problem is to take it one step at a time, as professionals do.

Index

© Ayan Chatterjee 2017
A. Chatterjee, *Building Apps for the Universal Windows Platform*,
DOI 10.1007/978-1-4842-2629-2

265

Get the eBook for only $5!

Why limit yourself?

With most of our titles available in both PDF and ePUB format, you can access your content wherever and however you wish—on your PC, phone, tablet, or reader.

Since you've purchased this print book, we are happy to offer you the eBook for just $5.

To learn more, go to http://www.apress.com/companion or contact support@apress.com.

Apress®

Printed in the United States
By Bookmasters